D1246553

Trial BY Fire

A Neurosurgeon's Conviction in Medical Missions

BERT PARK, M.D.

ACW Press
Eugene, Oregon 97405

Trial by Fire
Copyright ©2003 Bert E. Park, M.D.
All rights reserved

Cover Design by Eric Walljasper
Interior design by Pine Hill Graphics

Packaged by ACW Press
5501 N. 7th Ave., #502
Phoenix, Arizona 85013
www.acwpress.com
The views expressed or implied in this work do not necessarily reflect those of ACW Press. Ultimate design, content, and editorial accuracy of this work is the responsibility of the author(s).

Library of Congress Cataloging-in-Publication Data
(Provided by Quality Books, Inc.)

Park, Bert Edward.
    Trial by fire : a neurosurgeon's conviction in
medical missions / Bert E. Park.
      p. cm.
    Includes bibliographical references.
    ISBN 1-892525-98-4

    1. Christian life. 2. God--Will. 3. Discernment
(Christian theology) 4. Park, Bert Edward.
    5. Neurosurgeons--United States--Biography.   I. Title.

BV4509.5.P37 2003   248.4
                          QBI33-1092

Printed in the United States of America.

Contents

Indictments

⌐══✦══⌐

Dying to self, and depending on Jesus, transforms us into the likeness our Creator intended from the beginning.

⌐══✦══⌐

Pride and self-sufficiency offend God's sovereignty; humility and self-sacrifice engender His grace.

⌐══✦══⌐

Should we continue to ignore the Lord's call, He may declare war on our work and relationships.

⌐══✦══⌐

Only the works that God does through us--not those we do for Him--affirm His reality to servant and sufferer alike.

⌐══✦══⌐

Diligent service in the Lord's name is no substitute for a zealous search after His heart.

⌐══✦══⌐

Nothing affords greater personal and professional fulfillment than to reconcile what we do with what we were created to be.

Opening Arguments

Dying to Self

S an Salvador; 8:30 P.M.: I returned to my room, exhausted after having seen more than a hundred patients in the primary-care clinic that Monday. The night before, halfway through my first medical missions experience abroad, I had resigned myself to stay on for a second week with the Operation Blessing team in El Salvador. In effect, I was closing the door on a part of my life by canceling a speaking engagement in Washington, D. C. the coming weekend. Having carved a modest niche for myself in the academic community apart from neurosurgery, my about-face at the eleventh hour was certain to erase any credibility I had earned among my colleagues in history and political science. That price of discipleship, however, was "pocket change" compared to what the Lord had invested in me. Just as doors cannot be left half open in His Kingdom, a life lived for Him cannot be committed only in part.[1]

The early morning hours had been a sleepless vigil spent in unaccustomed prayer, arguing with God. Ultimately He prevailed on me to fulfill the entire commitment I had made by going to Central America in the first place. My prayers centered upon the Beatitudes from Jesus' Sermon on the Mount, the first verses I memorized following my conversion. I sought some direction—no, affirmation—from them now. Yet I could not divorce my thinking entirely from the expectations of why I *thought* I had been called to El Salvador. The operations I envisioned doing had not materialized. Rather, I was mired in the clinic seeing diseases a neurosurgeon is ill-prepared to diagnose, much less treat effectively.

This only magnified my fatigue through the endless day in 105° heat, and I relished the thought of a shower before tumbling into bed. Ruefully glancing at the phone that would sound tomorrow's 5:00 A.M. wake-up call, I was startled to see the red message light blinking ominously. Was one of my patients doing poorly back home? Could the convener of the conference be calling to lambast me (once again) for letting the participants down? Wearily, I picked up the phone. A recorded message conveyed a sense of urgency: I was to meet the team leader in the lobby the moment I returned. A neurosurgical emergency had arisen out at the plane, and I was needed there right away. "How could that be?" I thought. "They were only doing eye surgery—cataracts and the like—on our L1011 Flying Hospital that had been retrofitted with operating rooms. What need could they have for a neurosurgeon?"

On the fifteen-mile drive to the military airport (the only landing strip in El Salvador that could accommodate such a huge jet), we speculated as to what the emergency might be. Yet my thoughts were elsewhere, still ruminating on the fateful decision I had made the evening before. Were the Beatitudes a realistic life's view to have embraced, particularly now that they had practical consequences?

The music on the radio didn't help matters. "If I Were a Rich Man," the disillusioned Russian peasant, Tevye, waxed philosophical as we drove through the night. Well, I already was, at least by the world's standards—and that was a big part of the problem. I faced the same predicament as the rich young man in Matthew 19:16-22, who had accosted Jesus with the question that goads us all: "Good Master, what must I do to have eternal life?" This wannabe disciple had expected to hear some weighty pronouncement—not an absolute claim on his obedience. To his chagrin, and now my own, Jesus challenged us both to be done with academic arguments[2] and get on with the task of simply obeying.

"Sad irony," I remember thinking, "that the financial resources making this adventure possible were now being placed at risk." You see, there was far more at stake than my reputation as an historian and political reformer. Those were mere diversions from a lucrative neurosurgical career, and ones that had recently taken a back seat to concerns about my practice. Relations with my two partners had become strained. Following my born-again commitment to Christ eight months before, I had been branded as somewhat suspect.

Sure, I had changed—"transformed" may be the more appropriate term. My exuberance as a new child of God knew no bounds. In retrospect, I realized how naive I had been to present study Bibles to my two associates for Christmas. You could have heard a pin drop in the office that morning! "Where," the silence seemed to speak, "is the case of California wine we have come to expect?" My subsequent decision to spend two weeks of vacation time working in El Salvador rather than golfing in Arizona seemed to seal the matter: the partner they thought they had known for the past fifteen years had finally gone off the deep end.

And perhaps I had. The choice God made on my behalf was now thrusting me into professional purgatory on a darkened airstrip in the bowels of Central America, when I could just as easily have been driving to the E. R. back home on a far more routine (and reimbursable) emergency. Shuddering at the thought of what I might face on my return home, my thoughts were interrupted by the flashing red beacon of an ambulance at the airport gate.

I grabbed my medical bag and two soldiers with drawn AK47s motioned for me to climb aboard. A fleeting thought crossed my mind: "Was this some ruse for kidnapping an American doctor that would make newspaper headlines the next day?" Or, like the infamous Nero, was I fiddling while my empire of sorts burned back home? I was about to enter an unknown and forbidding world with no other guidance but the hand of God I had only recently grasped. Was His lead really strong enough to sustain me? Could I depend on Him to supplant the life I had left behind? Were His Beatitudes worth the cost?

It hadn't seemed that way in the beginning. Jesus had "upped the ante" with His Beatitudes by giving me a set of marching orders that superseded the Ten Commandments of His Father—laws that I couldn't possibly fulfill, because they are written on the heart. And my heart had been the loneliest of hunters, betrayed by its own excesses. As the Good Book says, "from the overflow of the heart the mouth speaks."[3] "Spoken like a modern-day Tevye," I remember thinking, "as the Old Order in Czarist Russia crumbled about him."

"On the other hand" (belying both of our tendencies to rationalize), how could either of us expect to have done any better than the Pharisees? Paying lip-service to a legalistic set of Old Testament laws was an exercise in hypocrisy; I had been guilty on every count at one point or another. Outward laws certainly hadn't changed me. They highlighted my obvious shortcomings, but offered no solutions. Like many of my neurosurgical patients, I needed an operation—one that penetrated to the heart of the matter in more than just the metaphorical sense of the word. After all, it's not so much the head as the heart that separates us from God.

If the Ten Commandments of the Old Testament are an inviolable set of absolutes that have been all but subverted by modern man's relativistic value systems (or lack thereof, as Tevye himself had discerned), the Beatitudes of the New Testament stand in diametric opposition to what the secular world subscribes to today. To what I subscribed to—until I viewed the wondrous cross through Jesus' eyes. The manner in which He bore His own cross extracted a life-changing confession: I had been walking the wrong path and not bearing my share of the load. Stepping out in faith into the missions field at last gave me clear affirmation that I had been inexplicably blessed on this road less traveled, albeit through no merit of my own. Awaiting me there was an encounter with God's Kingdom here on earth, and the blessings of the Christian walk— so long as my journey centered on the only cross that mattered: the cross of Calvary.

The lamp that would light my way was Jesus' Sermon on the Mount, the first didactic lecture Christ had given to His disciples. No mystery there; the very term "Beatitudes" means "blessed" or "favored." What favor could possibly be greater than God's blessing, this nine-fold prescription for living a life worthy of His calling? My quest followed a logical progression: from sight, through surrender, to faith; from "Are they true?" through "Am I willing to live by them?" to "Are they realistic for the role my Creator has designed for me?"

But first I had to undergo that painful operation—painful, because granting permission to allow my heart to be tinkered with was intensely personal. Its dark recesses concealed fears and doubts that had never been exposed to the light of day, much less the Christ-light. Acknowledging that conundrum triggered more spasms of remorse in the early going than hunger for righteousness! I was experiencing a full-blown "heart attack," though not of the kind one usually associates with the term. From Jesus' perspective, dying to self is like undergoing open-heart surgery: at that critical moment when the patient "goes on the pump," the heart stops beating. A power outside the body takes over as the surgeon does his work. If all goes well, a bad heart is made good, offering the initiate a new lease on life.

Despite Christ being my surgeon and the Beatitudes His operative manual, I vowed to become intimately acquainted with both before submitting my heart to His knife. This was akin to asking for some kind of informed consent, where the physician offers a proposition, spells out the anticipated result, and warns the patient of any potential adverse consequences. Yet before consenting to the experience, you have to believe in the surgeon Himself. Once done, you simply confess that you're at the end of your rope and cannot make it as you are on your own. Only then do you feel comfortable (convicted?) enough to take this leap of faith.

In anticipation of what lay ahead, I turned to the first page of the manual that defined the context in which the "surgery" would be performed and its intended result: taking a compromised heart and making it whole again. And mine, quite frankly, was on its last leg. The reputation earned through years of exhaustive work and the financial rewards of a busy practice had their limitations. How far had I come, and for what purpose, when others could compromise my professional standing to advance their own agendas? Hence the compelling need for a new set of heroes. Just as those "praise and worship" troubadours of my first life, Simon and Garfunkel, once rued the demise of the secular world's icons with that memorable line from "Mrs. Robinson": "Where have you gone Joe Dimaggio?" I now bid farewell to my own icon—the proverbial Renaissance Man.

Perhaps I should have read Ecclesiastes beforehand and seen the truth rather than to have gone deaf listening to my alter-ego. The prescription for change, after all, promised to be painful. For God's Kingdom turns the table upside down. Which is precisely what happened to me once I was called, with all the good and bad that implied. Yet such a difficult convalescence proved to be temporary. It's simply what one has to go through to make life whole. I shouldn't have been surprised, because the Lord had included in His informed consent an age-old Christian caveat: anticipate facing reversals immediately after experiencing spiritual highs. New Believers describe this as "going down into the valley to be tested." That's where the lilies grow.

What makes all of this so perversely difficult for the disciple is that the Lord gave us a new set of laws in the Beatitudes that are impossible for anyone to follow—and then commands us to keep them! That compels us to confess we can't possibly go down there alone. Yet once we surrender our self-absorption to a higher calling, we somehow manage to find our true selves—and God—in the process. It's our only way to serve Him, which is what we were made to do from the beginning. Dying to that old self—going down into the valley—we are reborn into God's Kingdom. That alone defines the meaning of our existence: self-actualization in accord with the divine plan of our Creator; that spiritual reality within us; why we are here; the purpose for which we are made. That's what Christ meant when He said "the Kingdom is now."

Acting upon this revelation is what makes Christians tick. What had I been searching for? Precisely what I was created in His image to do! To begin with, He had given me a challenging profession and some skills that cannot be accessed in some parts of the world. Yet for twenty years the allure of the secular world had blinded me to that elemental reality. Eschewing the life God had planned for me, I had stood proudly—and far removed—from where the Lord was working. That's why He declared war on my practice and, by extension, my professional relationships among those outside the Call. He had led me down into the valley.

This may be where the lilies grow, but some are adorned with thistles to mark the transition—what Paul described as his "thorn in the flesh." My own thorn was God's way of warning me that I was still on the wrong path. Our descent into the valley together by way of El Salvador now turned me in a different direction. That's why He had placed the Beatitudes in my hand the evening before as a road map to follow.

Jesus also provided me with a warranty deed—what I was guaranteed to encounter as a consequence of my journey. Mind you, that wasn't buried somewhere in the fine print! It was spelled out in bold type: *Persecution would be the price for becoming His disciple.* True, the beginning and end of the first eight Beatitudes offer the same redemptive promise: "for theirs is the Kingdom of Heaven." Yet living that here and now, reflecting the Christ-light, comes with a price in the secular world: "persecution because of righteousness." Not our own righteousness, to be sure; that is unearned. We are only made right in the eyes of God—"justified" is the precise term—by His Son's finished work on the cross. As such, the last Beatitude would read: "persecution because of [Christ's] righteousness [reflected in me]."

To be truly justified, then, implies being changed from without—Christ within you, yet "without" you. Once that happens, even the casual observer recognizes the born-again Christian is somehow different. And that promises disturbing consequences in the "real" world. Change can be frightening, particularly for others when it threatens their own sense of self. A frequently exercised option is to "quarantine" themselves, to avoid catching what C. S. Lewis termed the "good infection." As one measure of comfort for the Believer who finds himself so isolated, Jesus added a ninth and very personal Beatitude to His sermon (Matthew 5:11) to remind us that our predecessors—and Jesus Himself—had already suffered immeasurably more on our behalf. Hence the change from "blessed are those," found in every other Beatitude, to "blessed are *you*" (emphasis mine).

13

That comes, however, with yet another warning. Just as the apostle Paul had discerned, Jesus was personally alerting me of the spiritual warfare to come, for which I needed to put on the "full armor of God."[4] Providentially, that had been the second portion of Scripture I had memorized—and in fact had recited many times before undertaking difficult operations or facing the "slings and arrows" of my persecutors. I should not have been surprised. The Lord prepares us for what He knows we will face, whether in doing His work abroad or facing retribution at home. This was the first lesson I had drawn from my study of the Beatitudes. There would be many more to follow; and those began to unfold in El Salvador.

10:30 P.M.: Lying on the ambulance stretcher was a comatose child, intubated and supported by an ambu bag attached to his breathing tube. The faces of my colleagues reflected shock and disbelief. Eric, the poster child whom Operation Blessing had chosen in El Salvador as the symbolic beneficiary of the wonders of modern medicine, had undergone a brief anesthetic for a routine eye procedure to correct his crossed eyes. Inexplicably, he had suffered a cardiorespiratory arrest and now lay in a coma as a result of our team's best intentions.

As the ambulance sped through the gloom on its way to the national pediatric hospital in San Salvador, I was asked to monitor Eric's progress (or lack of it) as his new doctor in an ICU of Spanish-speaking medical personnel—with my patient attached to a primitive respirator and the reputation of our entire organization hanging in the balance. To be sure, there was nothing neurosurgical that could be done. Yet I was the only member of the team who had any working knowledge of neurology and respirators. The Lord had already anticipated the need; that's why He convinced me to stay on for the second week of the trip.

Nothing would make this tragic tale more gratifying than to report that Eric made a dramatic recovery. Such was not to be. Nor could his shell-shocked parents comprehend the magnitude of their loss in the early going. Unwittingly, our team chaplain contributed to their remorse by assuring them that God would heal their broken son. Certainly that did not square with my own expectations; I had seen far too many such patients to believe otherwise. What made this particular situation so difficult is that I was now their only medical link to the tragedy that had befallen them—a doctor whom they'd never met, but who was a part of the team that had brought them such misery instead of the blessings the name of our organization had led them to expect.

For weeks they slept fitfully on the stone floor outside the ICU, awaiting a miracle that never came. At week's end, I was mercifully rescued from this lingering purgatory when the time came for our team to return home. But not without ruminating over the implications of Christ's first Beatitude for everyone involved: "Blessed are the poor in spirit, for theirs is the kingdom of heaven." To my way of thinking, little Eric's kingdom had been converted to hell on earth.

I found my only comfort by recalling the Genesis account of Joseph, who had been sold by his jealous brothers into slavery in Egypt. Through many trials over the years, he ultimately found favor among the ruling hierarchy. As the Pharaoh's prime minister, Joseph had earned his trust and, in time, was rewarded by being reconciled with his brothers without any trace of revenge to despoil the reunion. "You meant it for bad," he had told his brothers, "but God meant it for good."[5] This was Joseph's way of telling them (and myself!), "Never judge God in the middle of your present circumstances."

I have no way of knowing whether Eric will ever improve enough to reconcile his own misfortune on this side of the Great Divide. But as a child of God on the other? By all means! That's what Jesus promised with His first Beatitude. Still, I couldn't help but feel that these children of God had every right to expect His blessing here and now. That too is a part of the promise. By the end of the day, each is promised to have discovered in his or her own way that theirs indeed is the Kingdom of Heaven here on earth—His indescribable peace that passes all understanding. As for myself, both the discovery and the peace took some time in coming.

Divine Appointments

The first thing you discover as a Christian, once you've been called down into the valley, is that you're not alone. Servant and dispossessed meet one another—and the Lord—on the valley road together. The servants are the more "favored" of the two; in the apostle Paul's words, they've been "chosen."[6] Perhaps my wife, Vicki, justified the use of the latter term most succinctly and intuitively when she said: "Only God knows which hearts He can change." Paul Azinger alluded to the same thought in his eulogy following the golfer Payne Stewart's untimely death and the transformation in his friend's life that preceded it: "Only God can change a heart like that." From Jesus' perspective, however, the cause is not nearly so important as the intended effect, which is in the giving. And that, you see, is what Christians are *chosen* to do.

Though some might object to the pretentious ring of the word "chosen" (as did I before studying Romans), of one thing there is no doubt: Christians have been favored by virtue of God's grace alone—and there's more than enough of that available through Jesus' finished work on the cross. God's grace flows out to those around them. That enables us to serve; for the only Christ that others "see" is a reflection of the Christ-light from His servants.

Lacking the natural advantages that most of us possess, the dispossessed turn by default to a higher power in time of need—which for them, is always. Jesus shares in their suffering and knows what it's like to be without. And if Christ's servant is privileged enough to meet such sufferers on the road, both lives will be changed immeasurably. This is the overriding theme of the Beatitudes: why the chosen are so blessed, and why the unlucky are so, well, lucky![7] The servant receives affirmation; the downtrodden, a reason to believe.

There is an old saying among Christians that the only arms the Heavenly Father has to embrace His children are our own. As for the Son, He is disguised among the poor of which the Beatitudes speak. Jesus surrendered His exalted position to walk among them, to experience the trials of man through the prism of God. Both He and they are there to be served. Consider the proverbial bag lady: Is she a burden on society, or an opportunity for God? How we respond to her illumines the condition of our hearts. If they're open, we discover that nothing can be quite so rewarding as *feeling* her greatest needs and then *fulfilling* them—because we're really serving Him. Therein lies the "double portion" that Christ's Kingdom affords: His riches here on earth and God's treasures thereafter in Heaven.

Through these "divine appointments," I began to appreciate the first of Jesus' Beatitudes: what it means to be "poor in spirit" when applied to medical missions work. In the words of my favorite Christian writer, Philip Yancey, the term "desperate" covers all the bases. Having nowhere else to turn, the dispossessed and disadvantaged often turn to God. That brings with it His blessing, because the Lord has already served notice throughout the Beatitudes that He gives preferential treatment to the poor.

What, then, you're probably asking, makes them so deserving of Jesus' concern? Their lack of pride is certainly high on His list. Hubris is the root of all sin, and sin separates us from God. Having nothing to "show" for themselves, they don't carry the excess baggage you and I do. To paraphrase Yancey, that doesn't make them more virtuous; but they have less of an inclination to *pretend* to be virtuous.

Through no fault of their own, the poor in spirit are naturally placed in a position that befits the grace of God. The downtrodden are dependent, simply because they have no choice in the matter. From the Father's perspective, that's to their advantage; being more interdependent, they expect (and receive) little from competition with others and much more from cooperation.[8] Yet their ultimate security rests with Him, not them. That's why they are willing to accept the Gospel as the Good News the Lord intended it to be.

Well acquainted with suffering, they're also used to waiting. Medical missionaries see both firsthand. Perhaps the most humbling aspect of what we do presents itself at the beginning of the workday. Whether in Latin America, Asia, or the Far East, the lines of sufferers patiently waiting to be seen are always huge. Cutting through this ocean of humanity as we make our way to the clinic entrance inevitably evokes awe and fear.

Awe, because most of them have been standing in line for twenty-four hours or more, many after walking miles to get there. By Hebrew standards, they personify the term "poor in spirit," meaning literally "to crouch down" or "make oneself low." They have nothing to lose by coming, because they have so little to begin with. What they invariably bring with them, however, is faith—blind trust that we have something to offer them in the way of a medical cure.

Which leads to the fear. Not only does the crush of bodies always seem so close to our bus that we legitimately fear running over someone; each of us harbors the fear that we might not meet their expectations. To be sure, we *do* have something to offer them: a gift that has eternal value far exceeding their physical needs. Yet at the beginning of the day, after waiting a seeming lifetime, that is neither their perception nor their desire. Invariably I am so humbled by their plight and what we can legitimately deliver that I find myself praying variations on the same theme: "Oh Lord, in your own way, please help us to meet their needs so their waiting will not have been in vain—that they not be disappointed in us, which would only reflect negatively on what and who You are."

Throughout the course of every mission trip I have taken, I never manage to suppress these raw emotions of awe and fear at the beginning of the day. What diagnosis will I miss? Which medicine will the pharmacy be unable to provide? How many children with cerebral palsy will I cradle in my arms as the "neurologic consultant," knowing that I can do nothing for them physically? Will my spiritual medicine fill the voids I will encounter that day?

At such times of doubt, the Beatitudes come to my rescue. For the Lord promised that the poor in spirit will always have His undivided attention, His medicine, His blessing. The latter applies as much to the servant as the dispossessed. As befits my skeptical nature, of course, I had to be convinced of all three. After all, my experience with Eric in El Salvador had been a harsh introduction to the missions field. Yet with that would come unforeseen blessings that Jesus chose to reveal in His own time.

⁰══✦══⁰

One such blessing stemmed from a divine appointment the Lord waited four years to bestow. I suspect that the delay had more to do with my own spiritual immaturity than His divine plan; God knows, I'm a slow learner. Despite my ever-present shortcomings as a missionary, however, His timing as a revelator is always perfect.

During my third mission to China, He gave me an opportunity to revisit the tomb of the terra cotta warriors just outside the ancient imperial capital of Xi'an. In truth, I had little inclination to return there, having already "reviewed the troops" six months earlier from an isolated platform reserved for heads of state and other such worldly principalities. Imagine, then, our surprise when we were ushered down into the pit where only hand-picked restoration technicians tread to view this eighth wonder of the world "up close and personal." That the heavily guarded, roped-off entry proved just wide enough for us to pass single-file to this crypt of clay soldiers seemed fitting: "Small is the gate and narrow the road," I remember thinking, "that leads to life" after death.[9] Not so the breadth of the Lord's revelations once we gained entry to the Qin dynasty's reconstruction of what that afterlife entailed.

Why had a handful of Christian missionaries been granted the unique privilege to walk such hallowed ground? The answer was obvious, albeit only in retrospect: our divine Gatekeeper had something He wanted to show us. I should have known that all along. Just ten months before, while on mission in the Ukraine, He had accompanied me through another narrow aperture to reveal Himself so that others might benefit. To fully digest what Jesus had to teach me in China requires a brief digression recounting that earlier lesson.

My Ukrainian colleagues had accompanied me one Sunday to the Pochaev Laura Monastery outside Ternopil to view their own sacred tomb. In continuous existence since 1240 A.D., the Holy Assumption Cathedral was one of only three Eastern Orthodox shrines that survived Adolf Hitler's wrath in World War II. The first Father Superior of the monastery, Saint Iov, spent the greater part of his life in communion with God by wedging himself through a tiny opening, praying for days on end with no food or water, in a cave dimly lit by a single candle. What are purported to be his "imperishable" remains now lie in a silver shrine just outside the cave entrance, venerated by the faithful who visit there daily by the thousands.

Ironically, I had been to Pochaev Laura the day before with the rest of our team. It was so crowded, however, that even getting close to the cave had been out of the question. Yet, just as would be the case in China, God had something He wanted to show my Ukrainian friend and his family, who were professed agnostics. We returned the next day with special permission not only to visit the shrine, but to crawl inside the Holiest of Holies of their patron saint. As always, God was in control. He had preceded us there so that I might share the Gospel in an environment tailor-made to catch their attention. For the claustrophobics among us, that was no small feat, as we discovered while slithering through the shoulder-width tunnel one by one to the altar beyond.

Emerging from the grotto after our shared experience, the official guide sensed a disturbing change in my friends' demeanors and attempted to refocus their attention on the sacred relics. Yet the neurosurgeon and his son were now more interested in the depiction of Christ's Passion on the opposite wall, vividly portrayed in seven beautiful murals. They, of course, had been there many times before—but ruefully acknowledged they had never noticed the murals, nor had they ever heard the Good News. Oh, how God opens doors—even though some may be smaller than man would like! Lest I miss the point, that is how He would prepare me for a reprise of this experience in China.

As mortal men, no doubt we all share the first emperor of China's preoccupation with life after death. His take on what the future held, to be sure, was far different than my own. Whereas the Believer's future is assured by Christ's finished work on the cross, the Chinese of that era (and any but the most inveterate communists today) envision the afterlife as a continuation of things as they were before one's passing. From the emperor's morbid perspective, that came with some disturbing implications. The same life he had lived (infamously, it should be said) proved a vainglorious and cruel deceit in death—surrounded by thousands of clay soldiers standing guard as the emperor would continue to lust, scheme, and rule in a manner of his own choosing. Stated a more familiar way for those who take God at His Word: "Where there is no law, every man does as he sees fit."[10]

Building a monument to that obsession had consumed thirty-eight years of the emperor's reign. In keeping with everything else that man does apart from God, however, it wasn't enough to assure him the immortality he craved nor protect him from the grave robbers he feared. The irony was not lost on those of us with eyes to see: here was an imperial guard of clay constructed to keep life out—much as the Roman guard around Jesus' tomb was dispatched, paradoxically, to keep death within. And neither, in the end, succeeded. Whereas Pilate had lamely instructed his charges to "go and make the tomb secure as [best] you know how," the emperor had decreed that his own tomb was to be sealed forever. That meant burying countless artisans alive to keep the location and its contents secret.

The inroads of time, of course, ultimately exposed his treachery. I couldn't help but reflect on the emperor's motivations and their implications as they would have appeared two thousand years later to the eminent Christian apologist, C. S. Lewis: "The natural life in each of us is something self-centered, something that wants to be petted and admired, to take advantage of other lives, to exploit the whole universe. And especially it wants to be left to itself; to keep well away from anything better or stronger or higher than it, anything that might make it feel small. For it knows that if the spiritual life gets hold of it, all its self-centeredness and self-will are going to be killed, and it is ready to fight tooth and nail to avoid that."[11]

Hence, I suppose, the need for an imperial guard; or so this overtly paranoid despot had perceived. Perhaps John 3:20 spoke for the realists among us as we viewed the cracked visages staring blindly in the shadows: "Everyone who does evil hates the light, and will not come into [its presence] for fear that his deeds will be exposed." The emperor's fears, in the end, were not unfounded. Within a week of their exposure to sunlight, the soldiers' brightly pigmented colors had flaked off and disappeared.

From the distant vantage point of my earlier visit, the terra cotta warriors had appeared remarkably well preserved—in keeping with the claim made by the Chinese media at the time of their discovery in 1974. Yet once having gained access to the pit (abyss?), these hallowed icons proved to be little more than hollow shells that paled in comparison to the original perfection of God's last and greatest creation. The obvious imperfections of mortal restoration, painstakingly sealed with plaster of Paris, were no match for the Touch of the Master's Hand. Not that we should boast.... Through no fault but our own, we too have become fragile vessels of clay that only Jesus can repair to perfection—and resurrect for eternity. The prophet Jeremiah intimated as much hundreds of years before, and Christ Himself subsequently reminded us: "Can I not do with you as [these] potter[s]? As the clay is in the potter's hand, so are you in my hand, O house of Israel."[12]

That brings to mind the lamentations of yet another prophet, who spoke not for an emperor but for God: "My people have committed two sins: they have forsaken me, the spring of living water, and have dug their own cisterns, broken cisterns that cannot hold water."[13] What God was reminding me of at that moment is that His Son came to earth to serve as an artesian well, quenching the

Believer's spirit with a never-ending supply of fresh water. Why would any man choose to substitute such a priceless gift with cracked, empty cisterns—or fragile icons, for that matter? An infilled Spirit, like an artesian well, does not dry up. Broken cisterns do. Man-made resources will fail us in the end, just as they failed the first emperor of China. Only the Creator, Who made man and every living thing, can provide sustenance that lasts.

Perhaps it was no coincidence, either, that the first imperial capital of Xi'an was built at the junction of eight rivers, which have since dried up. The weathered, dusty figures that stood before me spoke volumes to the parched environment. No one knows why the rivers disappeared. That remains one of the great geophysical mysteries of our time. Yet it's hardly a mystery to God, who foresaw the ongoing rejection of His Son in this region of the world until the last century—and with that, just perhaps, the desiccation of China's own "artesian" wells.

As we wandered among these partially restored skeletons of imperial mythology, I was reminded of Ezekiel's valley of dead bones. It was as if, at that very moment, "the hand of the Lord was upon me, [bringing me] out by the Spirit and setting me in the middle of a valley full of bones."[14] Could these "bones" of China's past live? I wondered, as He led me back and forth in the pit. Not in some vainglorious attempt to resurrect them, as Ezekiel had prophesied; that, of course, was impossible. But did God have someone else in mind—such as their cultural descendants, who came daily to pay homage to the same kind of relics that the Ukrainians had worshiped for centuries? Could they be resurrected by the blood of Christ out of this wasteland of hollow men? Yes, Lord; Yes! Fill them with your Spirit, so they might renounce the folly of ancient history and embrace a future of eternal life.

Hadn't the apostle Paul said as much to the Greeks in the book of Acts? "Men of Athens! I see that in every way you are religious. For, as I walked around and looked carefully at your objects of worship, I [found] an altar with the inscription: 'To an Unknown God.'" That was enough for both of us, albeit in different times and places, to proclaim: "The God who made the earth and everything in it is the Lord of heaven and earth, and does not live in temples built by human hands"[15]—much less in tombs of dead emperors. The take-home lesson for the Chinese, just as for the Greeks, was underscored by Paul himself: "From one Man He made every nation of man. . . so they would seek Him and perhaps reach out for Him and find Him." In other words, the narrow road always leads away from ourselves and toward Jesus.

That was then. This was now. Yet the message has never changed. Much as the terra cotta warriors had been arrayed in perfect formations, I was reminded with fresh certainty that God had placed His own troops in such strategic locations as central China for a purpose. Onward, then, Christian soldiers! For what we were standing with face to face was an allegory for officialdom throughout China's history. Just as the oppressed workers who had constructed this mortal myth were deprived of physical life, so too are the poor in spirit of China today being deprived of eternal salvation by those who stand guard against letting life in—while struggling (in vain, it should be said) to keep death without. Yet the Potter will have His own way in the end, adding just enough water to the mix to bring dead clay to life. That was Ezekiel's prophecy then, and Jesus' promise today: "If you have any thirst, let him come to me and drink" (John 7:37). That's living water only He can provide.

Emerging from the pit, I cast a lingering glance over the rows of imperfectly reconstructed icons. There was urgent work to be done: bringing real men to life in Christ during what little time remains of the Seventh Day of Creation—men made from the same clay, but now recreated in God's image. Such were His revelations to me, and the spiritual preparation preceding the trials that lay ahead.

First Witness

Theirs Is the Kingdom of Heaven

Four years earlier, the Lord had led me to Latin America to cut my "wisdom" teeth as a medical missionary. In other parts of the world it can be much more difficult to convince the poor in spirit that they will experience Christ's Kingdom in eternity, not to mention here on earth. Because of my experience in South and Central America, where the people's hearts are so open and their spirits so hungry, I was unprepared for what we would face in Albania two years later.

In one nominal sense alone I was prepared, having been advised that my neurosurgical instruments would be superfluous in ministering to the needs of the Kosovar refugees caught up in the horror of the Serbian pogrom orchestrated by Slobadon Milosevich. That was but small consolation for what proved to be the most distressing of some twenty-five medical missions trips I have undertaken during the past five years. Despite my inability either to meet their needs or fulfill my own commitment to the Lord, His boundless grace took me to the next level of affirmation—but not before confessing that I had failed them and nearly denied Him.[16]

You see, the refugees I ministered to were hardly interested in what my God had to offer. After all, they were Muslims—and the thugs responsible for their oppression were Greek Orthodox Christians. This was "ethnic cleansing" in the name of a triune God they had never comprehended to begin with, much less accepted. What use did they have for Jesus? Why would they even consider leaning on the everlasting arms of Christ my King? To be sure, the only "arms" with which the Serbian Christians embraced their Kosovar neighbors were not those proverbial extensions of the compassionate heart; the arms were of a different sort, brandished to murder their husbands and destroy their homes. If arms were used in the anatomic sense of the word at all, it was to strangle helpless and terrified Kosovar women, at worst, or as restraints during the course of raping them "at best."

All I could offer, then, was an empathetic ear to the horrifying tales these women and children had to tell. For these, by and large, were my only patients. Virtually all their husbands or fathers had either been shot in the fields or had mysteriously disappeared. Could Jesus provide these "poor in spirit" an answer for their suffering, or even a hand to hold onto in the dark night of their souls? Realistically, no. As for Allah, he had no answers either—only revenge, or cries of "Jihad," in keeping with the legacy of Islam now literally set aflame in the Killing Fields of Kosovo.

To compound the bitterness of the elderly (and frustrate any thoughts of martyrdom the young might have entertained), they were powerless to act—and I, equally powerless to assuage their anxiety and depression. As if to underscore the futility of our mission, the medications I had packed, including the antidepressants they so desperately needed, never arrived. They had been stolen, either in Italy before boarding a ferry that took us across the Adriatic or by customs officials in Albania to be sold on the black market. All I was left with was God's medicine—and at least here, perversely, that proved inadequate to meet their needs. Had I really believed I could explain to these poor in spirit the "why" so that they might somewhat endure the "how"? Is theirs to be the Kingdom of Heaven? For that, no Christian (at least on this side of the Great Divide) has an answer.

Contrast that experience with one of the poorest in spirit I have ever had the privilege of ministering to, in a shanty-town on the outskirts of Guayaquile, Ecuador. He had been triaged to my cubicle to treat his painful facial tic, for which the only effective cure was a medicine I did not have or an operation I could not offer. Disheveled and reeking of alcohol, he stumbled in clutching at his face as if laboring in vain to pull the eyeball from its socket. "Armed" only with what the Lord provided, I grasped his contorted face in one hand and a Bible in the other. As my hapless charge continued to grimace in pain, I frantically began reading out loud: "Jesus went throughout Galilee…healing every disease and sickness among the people…those suffering severe pain…seizures, and paralysis."[17] Over and over I recited the same verses. And louder and louder—as much to drown out his moaning as to "exorcise" the spasms. This created such a commotion that other members of the team began to filter into my cubicle, eventually swallowing the two of us in a bear-hug of intercessory prayer.

Slowly and (at least to my way of thinking) inexplicably, the spasms subsided— and then disappeared! I was as dumbfounded as my grateful patient, for I had never believed in (not to mention, *used*) the laying-on of hands as a means of obtaining immediate healing. His doubts had even deeper roots. He simply could not comprehend that Jesus might have had a hand in this. To my patient's way of thinking, such a pitiful life as his was unworthy of God's attention; by his own admission, "he had to change himself first" before turning to Jesus, much less ask for His help. At this point our interpreter began to sing in Spanish with a soft, soothing voice: "Come just as you are, Hear the Spirit call, Come receive Christ the King, Come and live forevermore."

The lyrics spoke to this forlorn soul far more powerfully than I ever could have done— about what it means to be "poor in spirit," and why the lost and suffering are so loved by Jesus. Swaying back and forth to the melody with eyes closed and hands raised, he was suddenly overcome and dashed out of the cubicle. That left us perplexed and, I don't mind admitting, a little deflated—until he brought back his wife and three children! At that moment, five very impoverished and dispossessed sheep, who had never found their way in this world, entered the gate of the Lord's pasture. And by week's end, husband and wife had taken a place alongside us as "runners" in the clinic, ministering to those that still remained outside the gate, so that they too might enter into Jesus' presence. Servant and sufferer had met one another on the road down in the valley, and ascended the mountaintop together.

Sometimes the Lord leads us down a road when and where we least expect it. One occasion entailed a literal mountaintop experience in the heart of Nicaragua, ministering to a subset of the population our medical team had not even targeted. That day we had encountered seven very defiant youths loitering across the dusty road from our makeshift clinic enclosure. They had been there since early morning, obviously with far too much time on their hands and, by outward appearances, more than enough malice in their hearts. Their presence was a worrisome distraction for our team, with their rough-housing and churlish behavior, pointedly standing apart from the rest of the village population, who had been humble enough to stand for hours on end in the oppressive heat waiting to be seen.

Every so often I would emerge from my cubicle, ostensibly for a break—in reality, to fathom what it was they were really up to. "Surely these roughnecks are beyond the pale," I remember musing self-righteously, "and certainly beyond the reach of our ministry." For all I knew, these were modern-day Sodomites of a sort, lurking outside the clinic entrance, perhaps with an eye to defiling a few of those angels unaware we were ministering to behind our gated enclosure.[18]

They remained there throughout the day, for reasons I could only imagine. "Odd," I thought. "Did the Lord have something else in mind for them?" Was their studied nonchalance indicative of an unspoken need? Should I stay where I was, ministering to those who were following the rules—or go outside and meet them where, just perhaps, God was working? Ultimately I resolved to call their bluff before the day was out—much to the chagrin of my youthful interpreter, who was roughly their age and certainly recognized "bad apples" when he saw them. "No, not those," he cautioned me. "It's simply too dangerous to meet them on their own turf. Stay within the fence where there's some sense of order. If God wants them to be ministered to, He'll compel them to register like everyone else."

For eight hours I heeded the counsel of man—and not the mind of God that was painting my own into a corner—continuing to minister to those within the gates. At length, however, and empowered by the Holy Spirit, I ventured outside with my frightened interpreter in tow. "A challenge awaits us—and them," I exclaimed with thinly-disguised braggadocio. In truth, I had no other plan than to depend on my Lord's assurances not to worry about what I would say, but simply to rely on Him to guide me.[19]

Venturing up to one of the toughs decked out in a stocking cap with a Chicago Cubs logo, I offered an obligate "high-five." That universal greeting among youths everywhere had the added merit of exposing the beaded power bracelet I was wearing, which I often use as a prop to tell the Gospel story. One of the others took the bait, and asked me what it was for. This was all the affirmation I needed to forge ahead.

But not before asking myself: "What would Jesus do in this situation?" More often than not, He answered one question with another when encountering opposition. Using my best imitation of Him who was now speaking through me, I responded with a question of my own. "What do you they think these people inside the fence have come here to receive?" The Sammy Sosa wannabe responded with a sneer, "To get some drugs!"

Nervous chuckles all around. Then silence. "Because they've been chosen to play your game," mocked another, with eyes diverted as he kicked at the dust.

"Perhaps," I responded. "Yet those who are truly chosen by the One who brought me here and gave me these beads to tell His Story are receiving something much more important: not drugs, but the Bread of Life."

More silence. That well-intentioned metaphor went right over their heads! Bemused (and amused) by my earnestness, they began whispering in Spanish to one another amidst more giggles and posturing. Despite this obvious misstep on my part, however, none had as yet turned their backs. Impulsively, I pointed to the first bead (a black one, signifying sin) and launched into an explanation of the story of salvation—that God had come to earth as a man to make them right with their Creator. The red bead was His blood that made it all possible; the white, the end result of His forgiveness that washes us clean.

Their surly facade began to crumble. That some gringo had taken the time to come out of his protective enclosure and meet these hardened skeptics where they were was mystery enough. It was apparent that few, if any, had taken much interest in their lives up until then. Yet my olive branch withered in comparison to the notion that someone far more important—none other than God's own Son—had not only taken their concerns to heart, but had given His life for their very souls!

That alone softened seven very calloused hearts. Antipathy gave way to curiosity. Soon they were all perched on a rock ledge in rapt attention as the remainder of His Story unfolded. Seizing the moment, I beckoned for seven bracelets and placed one on each of their wrists as I continued to talk. With their hands now clasped in a link of beads that positively glowed in the Christ-light, I went down the row reciting the Sinner's Prayer with each, beseeching the Lord to open their hearts to His message. And in the end, seven of God's children confessed to Jesus as their Lord and Savior!

Yet they still had to be fed. Much to the dismay of our pastor, who could barely disguise his disdain that I was perhaps sowing valuable pearls among swine, I distributed our remaining Spanish New Testaments. No doubt he knew his own people better than I. Perhaps the man was right. Once again, I have no way of knowing whether the seeds Jesus planted that day fell on the sun-baked road to be snatched up right away, or among thistles that would engulf them shortly after we left. That's His call to make. Yet this much I know for sure. At the end of the day, there they still sat, Bibles in hand, talking excitedly among themselves.

With the sun setting, we boarded the bus to leave. As I climbed aboard, my eyes met the ringleader, whom I had likened to Peter. He pointed upward and, with an all-knowing smile, nodded to me in affirmation. A chill ran down my spine, accompanied by a lingering image of that final scene from the musical *Jesus Christ, Superstar* when the troupe of actors had boarded the bus, leaving behind one of their own on the cross as the sun set. What had been their literary license then was Jesus' literal legacy now. It was a sacramental moment, and one which only the Lord, by His divine providence, could have orchestrated.

What had begun as a simple, if impulsive, act of peacemaking—extending a braceleted hand to those who disdained the work we were doing—brought seven of God's sons to where they needed to be. Not that they had met our man-made requirements for being ministered to, which was what registering in the clinic was all about. Yet God supersedes our legalism to meet the needs of those whom *He* (not we) has called. That had been His intent all along on a very special day in a dusty mountaintop village in Nicaragua.

They Will Be Comforted

Those who mourn are blessed in God's Kingdom, because they have Jesus' promise that they will ultimately find comfort. Soon after we left Nicaragua, I received word that He had just such plans in mind for little Eric and his family back in El Salvador.[20] As if to add to the pathos of our patient's plight, his mother and father had never married. God took that to heart—which is tantamount to saying He made the necessary amends to fit His divine plan. Due in large measure to their shared travail, the Lord united Eric's parents in marriage. What's more, He prompted us to build a house for the family that not only met our patient's medical needs, but gave his brothers and sisters amenities they had never known: a toilet, running water, and a refrigerator. Most enabling of all, the emotional support the family received (and the gracious manner in which they responded to it) became a profound witness for Christ's love. And the Lord was glorified, as a vibrant house of worship emerged in their "churchless" village.

Through God's grace, and from His perspective, Jesus provided some lessons and much needed affirmation for myself as well. As for the lessons, Eric's predicament underscores that the way people respond to tragedy is dictated in part by the culture in which they live. In America, for example, many such responses are less than ennobling. Here, the technology that kept Eric alive in the early going would be viewed as an economic and sociological disaster—not to mention the distressing legal ramifications such an inexplicable tragedy predictably evokes.

Yet for Eric's family in El Salvador, the new-found presence of Christ in their lives was all the affirmation they desired. Why? Because the dispossessed are willing to accept less than what the proud and self-sufficient require here at home when medicine has failed. Two years later, his mother put into words what they all had come to believe: "When we were the weakest, Jesus was the strongest." I appreciated where she was coming from, ruefully acknowledging that we had been powerless to offer any medical cure.

Now I realize the Lord kept me there that second week for a preordained purpose: to serve as a minister to the family far more than as a doctor; to be a Carer more than a Curer. God made a way when there seemed to be no way: He saw Eric through those first few days in an environment that was as forbidding to me as it undoubtedly must have been for Eric. For we both intuitively realized—or so I believe he could—that as two who languished together in the darkest of valleys, neither of us had anyone else to turn to but Jesus. Blessed indeed, then, were we who mourned—each in very different ways—because of His presence in our lives that fateful week in El Salvador.

◦━◆━◦

The same could not be said, at first glance, for Eric's suffering counterparts in Russia. For the putrefaction of decay that characterizes the former Soviet Union sifts down, unconscionably, to its children—perhaps more so in Siberia. As something of a parody of our Wild West, where the dispossessed and politically suspect always seem to end up by default, those who mourn the most in this destitute land are the children—and, presumably, the few parents who can still be found that mourn for them. Orphanages there are ubiquitous; street children even more visibly so. And for the youngest, victimized by a whole host of congenital anomalies spawned by inadequate perinatal nutrition and alcohol in expectant mothers, there are no shunts available to treat the hydrocephalus ("water on the brain") that is so prevalent.

Though we had been warned by the Russian authorities that our mission there was to be medical and by no means "spiritual," the Lord blessed me with enough courage to pay lip service to the regime and still manage to speak the Good News to the people. At first subconsciously (yet by the end of our stay there, intentionally), prayer became my *modus operendi* in Siberia. Regardless of why I was told I was there, I had my own agenda.

That it was to be Jesus' agenda as well became apparent during the first pediatric clinic on the day after our arrival. I had been asked to consult on some thirty-five children with various stages of untreated hydrocephalus. To comprehend the magnitude of the problem, that's far more than any neurosurgeon is likely to see in his or her practice in a year. Their plights, and those of the parents who bore their burdens stoically (while responding to me, at least initially, in the same way) were so heart-rending that prayer became a natural extension of each examination I ministered. Knowing that I had brought only twelve shunts sharpened my diagnostic acumen as to which children would benefit from shunting, and which would not. For the remainder, God's grace had to suffice. Yet that, as ever, proved more than adequate for what He had in mind.

As I anticipated, praying with each of the families after examining their child and making recommendations raised a few eyebrows in the beginning. My Russian colleagues would respond by making a pretense of shuffling through the medical record or searching for the next set of Xrays while I indulged in such heresy. After all, that was a job reserved for the Russian Orthodox priest— and certainly only while in church! Yet half-way through the afternoon I began to sense the presence of shadows gathering behind me during my prayers. And by the end of the clinic, the three Russian neurosurgeons were self-consciously joining in the prayer circle, hands linked with mine. The presence of the Holy Spirit in those circles was palpable, as was His grace. You see, planting seed was all that the Lord legitimately expected of me; reconciling each of them to Himself was something He would take care of in His own time.

From a strictly professional perspective, my surgical experience during the first leg of our Siberian mission was more than I could ever have managed on my own: seven aneurysms clipped, two tumors resected, and four shunts successfully placed in but ten days. That was His reward, I believe, for ministering to His children. However, with our transfer from the large regional referral center in Krasnyorsk to the much smaller city of Bradsk the third week, it soon became apparent that I needed to be doing something besides operating. What few cases that remained there were put on terminal hold pending approval from some unnamed bureaucracy, or (more than likely) reserved for the single neurosurgeon, who remained far less hospitable than my colleagues had been in Krasnyorsk. I therefore resigned myself to the primary-care clinic, assuming my Provider had His own plans for me there.

My assignment was to be even more "primitive"—if ultimately more fulfilling—than I could have imagined. I was given the unenviable task of making house calls, visiting shut-ins who had no way of making it to the clinic, much less stand in an endless line waiting to be seen. Jesus opened that door in His own ineffable way through my good friend, Sebastian Sosa, whom I had first met four years earlier in El Salvador, and who was now serving as my interpreter.

That was no more of a coincidence than what our initial meeting had portended. After introducing himself, Sebastian casually volunteered that he was from an Argentine missionary family serving in Byelorus, and had been given the opportunity to attend Evangel College, a small Bible school in Springfield, Missouri. "Had I ever heard of it?" he asked. "I knew them both intimately," I had replied with a chuckle, "because I lived there!" Our friendship burgeoned during the next four years, though I lost track of him after his graduation—only to find that we had both volunteered to go to Siberia with Operation Blessing. Just another one of His coincidences, I'm sure....

Yet I digress from the real story to tell. It so happens that Sebastian had been visited by an elderly man in the clinic in Bradsk, who had come on behalf of his bedridden wife. She had been confined to her bed for eight years following a severe stroke, and her husband was now seeking a neurologic specialist to visit her in their apartment. Unable to walk or use her left side, she had not so much as seen the other two rooms of their cramped living quarters for almost a decade. That would have been the harshest purgatory imaginable had her loving husband not tended to her day and night through the years, propped up in a wooden chair for hours on end next to the bed, ministering to her every need.

Sebastian sought me out and we agreed to go there immediately, accompanied by a nurse who, to our eternal debt, was simply "on fire" for the Lord. On the way out to the apartment, she prepared us spiritually for what she prophesied would be an exorcism of sorts by repeating over and over verses from the second chapter of Acts: "Suddenly a sound like the blowing of a violent wind came from heaven and filled the room where [the disciples] were praying. They saw what seemed to be tongues of fire that separated and came to rest on each of them. And they were filled with the Holy Spirit." In a matter of minutes, we three modern-day disciples would be a party to this description of Pentecost revisited.

On our arrival we were ushered by the husband into a tiny bedroom just large enough for a bed and a chair. A single window (barred, in keeping with virtually all apartments in Siberia) was their only visual contact with a world his wife no longer inhabited. There we began to pray over this destitute figure lying crumpled on the bed before us. I laid my hands on her head and paralyzed side, beseeching, by the blood of Jesus, that she be comforted.

Yet the nurse intuitively sensed as we prayed that the Lord had something greater in store. At length, she cajoled the woman to stand, despite my own more realistic and sobering concern that our patient might fall and break a hip—leaving her in worse condition as a result of our ministrations, and jeopardizing the credibility of the entire team.

Tentatively, she took her first step as the others clung to her and continued praying in the Spirit. They stood there, as if in suspended animation, for what seemed an eternity, teetering back and forth. As for myself, a Doubting Thomas, I crouched down below in anticipation of the inevitable fall. And then, with a flourish of defiance, she let go of their shoulders and limped off into her kitchen that she had not seen for eight years! With her paralyzed arm (to which I, the "expert," had already attested), she reached into a cabinet and grasped a jar of jam, thrusting it into my hand as a gesture of thanks with tears of joy streaming down her face.

Somewhere from the back of the room I heard the voice of God's prophet intoning in affirmation: "I saw the Lord always before me. Because He is at my right hand, I will not be shaken...my body will live in hope, because You will not abandon me to the grave."[21] It was the most sacred of moments. Through our interpreter we learned that the elderly woman's grandmother had told her something about God before the communist takeover. That's why her husband had dutifully sought out a priest from the Russian Orthodox Church when she had been felled by the stroke, telling him that his wife was seeking God's blessing to heal her. Could this Holy Man intercede for them? The priest had replied: "Once your wife is strong enough to come to church and light a candle there, then God will offer His blessing...."

Our grateful, if perplexed, patient had no inkling that the Divine Healer might seek her out in her own apartment! That God would "lower" Himself to visit her there was a far cry from what she had been taught by the religious establishment. Yet the Holy Spirit blows wherever it pleases, and takes us where the world cannot go. At that very moment she was being personally ministered to by His Son, Jesus, who had come into this world two thousand years before to break down such man-made barriers between God and His children. Now, in a squalid apartment in the heart of Siberia, He had made good on that promise of the Beatitudes to comfort those who mourn, where they are.

They Will Inherit the Earth

As for the meek, to them the Lord gives more than comfort; He promises that they shall "inherit the earth." Yet this, the third of His Beatitudes, comes with a warning to the servant: God may open doors; but man can still close them. That's a lesson I believe in retrospect our organization failed to heed on the maiden voyage to El Salvador of our L1011 Flying Hospital five years ago. Amid the fanfare of a boisterous reception complete with military band, a president who was using our arrival as a crutch to bolster his sagging popularity, and the crush of our own ever-present media, Eric's inheritance here on earth was lost. That was obviously not our intent; yet our pride got in the way. There was a certain air of Yankee "can-do" self-assuredness in our step, rather than the meekness of servants simply seeking their Lord's guidance.

It is certainly not my place as a volunteer for Operation Blessing to air its dirty laundry. However, many naysayers within the organization had already voiced fears of losing our focus on primary care in this rush to display the "ultimate" venue for medical missions work. No doubt, as a very visible instrument that has opened doors to areas of the world we might never have gained access to, the plane has been a plus. Yet the question arose then—and has continued to fester to this day—was it God who opened those doors, or simply the plane? Had it been His blessing that brought us to El Salvador, or the pride of American ingenuity—being so sure of ourselves that we targeted those children in advance through the media to receive the benefits of the Flying Hospital?

Our shared misfortune reminds me of a story found in chapter 4 of 1 Samuel following the capture of the Ark of the Covenant by the Philistines. The prophet Samuel had warned God's chosen people that the descendants of their chief priest, Eli, would suffer because his sons "had made themselves contemptible in the eyes of the Lord" and Eli had failed to restrain them. God spoke through Samuel about the devastating effects of sin in a corporate sense, the root of which is invariably pride. Not just the guilty paid the price, but the extended family and community as well. Neither sacrifice nor offering could atone for that. Eli and a host of other family members died, leaving his daughter-in-law alone to give birth to a son whom she named Ichabod, meaning "the glory has departed." The name underscored the loss of God's blessing and presence among the self-serving and prideful, when humility and obedience (a. k. a. "meekness") was all the Lord required.

I, for one, believe it was the absence of humility and obedience, far removed from the sacrificial offering of a plane that we proudly made on the Lord's behalf (with or without His blessing), that perhaps explains an otherwise inexplicable tragedy. Despite our best intentions, Eric was divested of his promised inheritance here on earth. A little more meekness on our part may have served him better. Yet if there is an upside to this (and one that admittedly diverges from the fate of Eli's descendants), it is that the Lord was ultimately glorified in our scramble to supplant what pride had wrought. His seed, albeit at Eric's expense, was planted deeply in the hearts of those who were impacted by the tragedy. And that has continued to grow to this day, nurtured by the humility and meekness that come naturally for the poor and dispossessed, so that others might inherit His Kingdom here on earth.

Not that I myself have completely taken that lesson to heart even now. It's difficult to point fingers at any organization of which you are but a volunteer, particularly when pride in your own skills so often deafens the ear to those plans God has in mind. If the laying on of hands and intercessory prayer to heal a painful facial tic in Ecuador or to rehabilitate a stroke victim in Russia (when I thought I should be doing neurosurgery!) had not been enough to alert me to my own hubris, yet a third encounter with God in South America continued to hammer home His message.

In Brazil the Lord convinced me that a full embrace will make amends should the hand alone falter—whether that entails a failed operation, or a laying on of hands in the absence of faith. We had encountered such spiritual warfare in the operating room at the local hospital in Brasilia trying to get cases done that I resigned myself to returning to the primary care clinic. If the truth be known, Jesus sent me there simply because the Divine Healer had something He wanted to teach me.

We had been in the clinic only an hour when a distraught mother burst into my cubicle with her son in tow—that in the most literal sense of the word, as the boy was actively convulsing. This was but one of several grand mal seizures he had experienced through the early morning hours as they had huddled together in a driving rainstorm amid a cast of hundreds awaiting our arrival. Yet once he began to choke on his own secretions and turned blue, the mother's meekness dissipated; she broke through the registration barrier to the examining stations inside. Mine just happened to be nearest the entrance. I'd like to think that was no coincidence in the Lord's scheme of things, as I was the one doctor there with the requisite "credentials" to treat epilepsy. Never mind that intravenous anticonvulsants are the only medication capable of arresting such repetitive seizures completely—and that we did not have. So much, then, for one's training and hard-earned degrees!

Impulsively, I grabbed the child and held on for dear life, as if I might somehow physically restrain his life-threatening rigors. A circle of support staff formed around the two of us, emitting a cacophony of prayer that gave new meaning to the term "Tower of Babel." They continued to pray—and I continued to wrestle—locked in mortal combat with a "demon" one-third my size, whose strength for the moment easily matched my own. Five minutes into this bizarre spectacle, I felt the boy go limp in my arms. Would that this have been a "simple" case of demonic possession, and I the exorcist! Yet my medical training told me otherwise. "My God," I thought, "we've lost him!" For as virtually all these patients eventually do, he had probably lapsed into a coma as the seizure ran its course before heralding the onset of the next. If so, he urgently needed an airway, and I prepared to lower him to the ground to begin CPR.

Yet a strange thing happened on the way to my first "Code Blue" in the missions field. Perhaps I should have taken more notice of the distinct impression I had that something *fled* the boy's body at the moment he "collapsed" in my arms. As I released my grasp and called for an endotracheal tube, he simply opened his eyes, blinked—and then walked over to his weeping mother with arms outstretched. There he curled up meekly in her lap, yawning and staring at this huge entourage of strangers, as if we had interrupted his afternoon nap.

The seizures had stopped and then vanished without a trace—despite no medicine except "arms around" (as opposed to "hands on") prayer—and absent any of the residual side-effects doctors invariably see following repetitive seizure activity. Far less worse for wear than the rest of us, the little boy reached into the pocket of his mother's shabby jacket and pulled out a plastic race car. Oblivious to our presence, he knelt down in the dirt and began pushing it around in circles—and then, right out the door....

I never saw them again. Yet the parting image still lingers: that of a mother who had just had a pearl of inestimable value returned to her for safekeeping; and a boy who behaved as if the world was his oyster. And so it was. That was his inheritance the Lord has promised the meek.

On my own behalf I received a strong dose of humility—as if Jesus was bringing me "down" to their level of meekness so that I might inherit also. I can still hear Him at the end of that fateful day in the clinic, which had begun with myself sulking in a blue funk because the operations scheduled had been postponed: "My son, there's a world of difference between a surgeon and a servant. Do it your way, if you like; but you'll do it alone. We've been here before. How many times do we have to take this walk around the desert? Mind you, this is my clinic, and we'll do things *my* way!"

Blessed are the meek, for they shall inherit the earth. Plus humility and the hereafter—the inestimable value of which the Lord had once again affirmed inside a dusty warehouse in Brazil.

They Will Be Filled

I f ever there were a people that hungered for righteousness
and were filled accordingly with the fruits of the spirit in
the most literal sense of the word, it would be the farm families of
Almolonga, a small town nestled in the western highlands of
Guatemala. As so often happens in medical missions work, however, their story (and ours) began with a reversal of fortunes. It
had been another case of God opening a door—and man,
through his own ineptitude or cynicism, closing it just as quickly.
That's how our team ended up in Guatemala rather than Cuba.
Nothing more than a tactical blunder, to be sure. We had the great
fortune to have been invited to Cuba to pave the way for a much
larger mission there later in the year, but we inadvertently
slammed the door on that opportunity by sending all of our medical supplies in advance of the team. Now, Fidel Castro is nothing
if not a pragmatic man. Having the medicines Cuba sorely
needed—and now able to eschew the Christian message that was
to be the price paid for our admission—the Ministry of Health
simply "disinvited" us two weeks before we were to embark.[22] It
was a devastating blow.

Being "all dressed up and nowhere to go," as it were, our sponsor hastily arranged an alternative missions trip for the team members, who had already scheduled valuable time away from their work. Through the Lord's grace alone, we managed to link up with a church in Quezaltenango, Guatemala, and arrived there late Saturday.

As a "Type A" surgical personality, I always chaffed at such down-times before beginning work—which in this instance would be the following Monday. How, then, to spend Sunday? That brings me to Almolonga, one of three locales in the world featured in an inspirational video entitled "Transformation." As an abiding witness to the blessings the Lord bestows on those who hunger for His righteousness, theirs was a reversal of fortunes with eternal ramifications. For none had been so richly and visibly blessed as this farm village of ten thousand inhabitants, located just ten miles from where we were staying.

More out of curiosity than anything, the team elected to spend Sunday there. After viewing evidence on the tape of the Lord's ongoing presence in Almolonga, I was more than curious—"rabid" would be an apt description! That would afford a huge measure of the affirmation I had been seeking all along, as one still caught up in a Christian walk guided as much by sight as by faith. We all received affirmation in spades before the day was out—not to mention something far more important, which was responsible for the astounding success of our brief mission there.

I'm speaking of the privilege of being anointed by a true man of God, who prepared us spiritually for our appointed task. To understand that requires acquainting the reader with what had happened in this heretofore nondescript farming community. Let me briefly recount their remarkable story.

Thirty-five years ago, an unemployed Mayan's life was changed forever and, by extension, the town where he had spent a lifetime. Out of the blue, God spoke to him one day, bemoaning the idolatry that gripped Almolonga, where alcoholism was rampant, the jails were full, and the men refused to work. What few crops they planted were left to rot in the stagnant environs that resembled a modern-day Sodom and Gomorrah. God had taken their perfidy to heart. That's why He commanded this most unlikely disciple to pray and fast for a revival in Almolonga, a community split between pagan Mayans who literally paid homage to a wooden cowboy, and Catholics who worshipped icons in the local cathedrals by day and then staggered off as night fell to resume drinking in one of the town's thirty bars and saloons.

Night and day for months, he fasted and prayed alone on the hillside overlooking his hometown: "In the name of Jesus, take this demon possession of idol worship out of them!" At length he received enough affirmation to brave returning to the town center, where (through no power of his own) three miracles occurred in quick succession that literally transformed Almolonga overnight. The first was the exorcism of a demon from the town's certified "crazy man" in full view of neighbors who had mocked both of them for years. The second was the healing of a paralytic in the name of Jesus. And the third was a miracle of Lazarus-like proportions: a woman brought back to life, who was certified to have been dead as a result of gangrene after a botched C- section. What makes these miracles so compelling (shades of the empty tomb!) is that all three are alive and well today, members of the huge Christian church this chosen man of God now pastors.

Yet that's just a small part of the story. Overnight, a revival began that united all churches—Christian, Catholic and even pagan—under the banner of Jesus Christ. The town was transformed. Men returned to the fields; alcohol disappeared; bars (and jails!) closed. On account of that, the fruits of the Lord's harvest became a wonder for all to see. Before, three or four trucks of produce a month had made the trip to market in Guatemala City, four hours away. Now, more than *fifty* truckloads per *day* leave this bustling township, filled with vegetables whose size and quality defy scientific explanation: carrots two feet long; radishes and cabbages larger than basketballs and so heavy that both arms must be wrapped around one just to be able to carry it!

More affirming still, these crops are grown on some of the most difficult terrain imaginable, with steep slopes that make farming tenuous at best—and where neighboring villages that have not experienced a revival in Jesus' name continue to eke out little more than a meager existence. For, you see, the town of Almolonga alone among these is Christian to the core. And not just nominally so; church services throughout the week are packed with Believers. Indeed, the entire life of the community is built around them.

That Sunday we attended three services at different times and locations during the late afternoon and early evening. The third church is where we met the chosen man of God who, as Jesus' instrument, had been "responsible" for it all well over a quarter-century ago. What struck me about this divine healer was that, as a human figure, there was nothing noteworthy or appealing about him. If anything, he was decidedly *uncharismatic*. On that basis alone, I remained skeptical of his alleged powers—that is, until the time came for him to confer the Lord's blessing on our mission in Guatemala.

One by one, a power outside this man dropped my friends to the floor at the touch of his anointing hand. Sensing my own skepticism, he passed me by time and again as he ministered to the other members of the team, now littering the floor like so many limp rags. Now, I don't mind admitting that this whole exercise was something I both disbelieved in and actively resisted—until, like the others, I found myself helplessly dropped to the ground by the mere touch of his hand on my forehead. One of the members of the team described in her own inimitable fashion what happened on that Sunday: "Well, I guess we all went church-hopping until everyone finally got drunk!"

Never had I been privileged to witness the fruits of the Spirit so literally as I did in Almolonga. That carried over to the entire mission for the remainder of the week. What had transformed this farming community steeped in idolatry and alcoholism has no explanation other than the Lord's abiding presence. And I, the greatest skeptic of all, had been empowered by His touch through a man of God, who had been chosen against his will. Rather than chaffing under the boredom of a "down" day before we began work, the Lord had led us through an intense afternoon and evening of spiritual preparedness, the likes of which none of us had ever conceived— much less partaken of—before ministering to the poor in His name.

The result was a clinic experience that set records for Operation Blessing, which in numbers alone will probably never be surpassed: in only five days, nine doctors both treated and minis-tered to over 3,500 patients. Surgically, I witnessed results that defied the odds in such a primitive setting: an all but blind young man with cysticercosis of the brain (a tapeworm infestation) that I shunted, who inexplicably regained his vision; a woman with a perversely recurring brain tumor that had been operated on unsuccessfully on four separate occasions, who finally had it com-pletely removed; an anesthesiologist at the local hospital (and a classical guitarist by avocation), who was left without any dis-cernible deficits in his dominant hand after having a treacherous nerve sheath tumor resected without benefit of an operating microscope. None of this could have been possible without the Lord's presence there and our intense spiritual preparation the weekend before.

Far more important, over half of the 3,500 patients we treated in the clinic gave their lives to Jesus in the process of having their physical needs met. Those were small potatoes compared to the table of plenty the Lord had prepared. For God knew that each in his or her own way hungered for a righteousness that only the Divine Physician could satisfy. Just as King David had discovered in a far different place and time, it was the *seeking* that made all the difference—as in "seeking after God's own heart." Whereas the care-givers had their way prepared by seeking out the Lord's proven disciples among His own people, the care-receivers were simply seeking to be filled. And for those with open yet empty hearts, the real Doctor never disappointed.

Nothing underscored this more than the testimony one of our team physicians from Mexico gave to the group the night before we left. By everyone's admission, Dr. Ariel was the most diligent of the physicians there. He had spent an inordinate amount of time the first three days painstakingly examining each patient he saw, and giv-ing them the best medicine we had to offer. Yet by his own admis-sion, Ariel was perplexed by the fact that when he would emerge from his cubicle to call for the next patient, many of those waiting said they preferred to see one of the other doctors. His curiosity aroused, our friend peeked into the other cubicles to see what his colleagues had to offer that, by word of mouth among those waiting in line outside, captivated them so. What Ariel saw were doctors and nurses huddled with their patients in prayer. As he so humbly put it: "They didn't want the medicine I had to offer; they were hungry for the Lord's medicine. That's why they had come."

"Blessed are those who hunger for righteousness; for they shall be filled." That was the take-home lesson for servant and poor in spirit alike during this brief but bountiful harvest the Lord had arranged in Guatemala—despite man having closed the door on what was thought to have been a missed opportunity for Him elsewhere. Only Jesus can provide such affirmation, in a place and time of His choosing, among those who seek His righteousness above all things.

Recess

Reality Check

This matter of thirsting for righteousness in the Lord's service occasionally has its downside from the secular point of view. One of the reasons the Beatitudes caught my attention so soon after coming to Christ is that they mirrored my own experience juxtaposed to what the "real" world values—when all I had been looking for was affirmation of the reality of Jesus in the lives of other Christians. Yet another motivation was admittedly more egocentric: affirmation of my own self-worth. Though a far less laudable goal than the first, it remains a driving force for Believer and agnostic alike.

What I'm tangentially referring to is reward. Whether one terms that an "inheritance" is a matter of perspective. On one thing, however, virtually all agree: to banish all motivation of reward (or of at least avoiding punishment), either in this life or the next, is to render our existence a meaningless, existential exercise. The only choice for those outside the faith is to have one's reward "paid in full" from society now in one lump sum, in contrast to Believers, who also receive a return on the principal: God's firstfruits here on earth, and His treasures in heaven forevermore.

I was confronted with that choice sooner than I would have liked. At this pivotal time in my life, when the Lord was turning my table upside down, opportunists from the secular world scrambled for the scraps that fell to the floor. What ephemeral rewards I had obtained financially, or "memorials" I had built by way of professional reputation, were taken from me in the blink of an eye by people I had come to trust.

It was, perhaps, a fitting end to the pretension that had characterized my original life's view as a Renaissance Man. All the more fitting because the alter-ego of my pre-Christian existence, a college professor by the name of Reynolds Price, had warned me of the pitfalls of placing one's faith in other people—in particular, catering to the false praise of men seeking to advance their own agendas. Price had been a professor of literature at Duke University when I was there as an undergraduate back in the Dark Ages of the sixties. The undergirding thesis of his life's view was that man should seek affirmation only in his work, because personal relationships are bound to disappoint in the end, casualties of deception, divorce, or death. I swallowed that view "hook, line, and sinker" for the next twenty years, and eventually came to appreciate where Price was coming from.

What I did *not* bank upon, however, was that my work was subject to the same vilification. That became manifest immediately after declaring myself for Christ—which, parenthetically, is the type of setback Jesus had warned His disciples would befall them. Christians call that the "cost of discipleship." What made this all so ironic is that a year or so after being reborn (and long after I had lost track of Professor Price), I discovered that my mentor had abandoned his own cynicism for a more virtuous perspective. One of the many books God put in my hands at that particular time was Price's *Three Gospels*. This reflected a quarter-century of his own search (and those of his students) for the historical Jesus, much as I had found myself doing over a briefer period of time before exchanging a head-full of knowledge for a heart of worship.

That, I now believe, was no accident. Long ago, God had placed us both on similar paths, knowing that our respective pilgrimages would ultimately lead us to the same end point—the reality of His

Son. After all, only the Lord knows which hearts He can change, and both of ours were on His list. By seeking affirmation in an environment far removed from mine, Reynolds Price's quest eventually dovetailed with my own: two shepherds of a sort, serving their respective flocks in very different ways, who met Jesus face to face on a road less traveled by academicians and physicians alike.

What we both had discovered after a number of false starts is that the Lord's offer—and our reward—centers upon a love relationship between Father and child. That's a far cry from the praise (even affection) that men extend to one another in the workplace, which usually rings hollow and is always subject to withdrawal. Such cannot be the case for God's divinely sanctified relationships, because Christ's love is *unconditional*—much like those endearing friendships of childhood, the likes of which are rarely recaptured as adults. Even when we fail Him, He's always there.

Out of gratitude for the ultimate price He paid on our behalf, any affirmation the Christian seeks is based on the approval from the one loved—in this instance, Jesus. By way of contrast, those who actively seek the approval of mankind during this lifetime have already been given their reward. Yet the beauty of Christ's offer is that the Christian receives a double portion: His promise of affirmation now and eternal life thereafter. It's a win-win situation, one that speaks to the very heart of Jesus' unmerited gift to the Believer: "Seek ye first the Kingdom of God, and all these things will be added unto you."

That promise was put to the test following my return from one of my earlier missions trips. Waiting for me on my desk was a letter from my two associates dissolving our partnership of fifteen years. Thereafter (and in league with a third neurosurgeon whom I had mistakenly taken at face value as a professed Christian[23]) they conspired to destroy my practice—and nearly succeeded. Was this the just reward that the meek were to inherit in the Lord's service? If ever I needed affirmation on God's terms, and not man's, it was now.

Jesus ultimately made good on His promise, because He knew He had my heart. He immediately called me to Nicaragua, where a whole host of rewards awaited me and, by virtue of the work I had been entrusted to do, a windfall for His Kingdom here on earth as well. For those two weeks produced a rich harvest on the Lord's behalf through no merit of my own—though more than adequate for myself by way of affirmation.

Along the way, He also provided a fellow pilgrim with whom to share a love of missions work, a few triumphs, and many more travails. Through his own Christian walk and mature witness, Mark Axness reconciled my professional losses with the spiritual rewards I had received. Both of us were being tested, yet God provided a soul mate to bear the load. Being equally yoked in shared adversity is entirely consistent with Jesus' very nature: by knowing beforehand that we will experience hardships and even persecution for His sake, the Lord will never give us more of a burden than we can bear—or share.[25] What He *does* give us in return, as Father to child, are those long-lost, unconditional friendships of youth.

That comforting bit of Scripture and its affirmation were put to an even greater test over the next six months as I balanced the rigorous demands of solo neurosurgical practice, absent cross-coverage, with subsequent missions trips to Ecuador and Brazil. Despite having been pushed from the nest amidst whispers swirling about me in the hometown where I had grown up, the surgical volume of my practice only increased, much to my former associates' dismay. To be sure, by virtue of my coverage predicament, I was unable to take any time off. From Jesus' perspective, of course, that was not nearly so important as the impact it threatened to have on the commitment I had made to Him.

Consequently, He made a way where there seemed to be no way by covering for me Himself. It was His way of saying, "Bert, you're going to far off places to shepherd the sheep of My pasture; for that, I'll take care of your own flock in return, and we'll see to it that it grows during your absence!" I had no greater comfort and affirmation than Jesus' very words: "Blessed are you when people…persecute you…because great will be your reward…."[26] By obeying the Lord's call and going where He was working, I was promised to have all my worldly needs and concerns—and, more important, those of my patients— provided for as well.[27]

In exchange for having lost the financial security of a group practice in which virtually 100 percent of the patients were medically insured, I had been given an inheritance of inestimable value. What's more, I was now able to minister to my patients in a manner of the Lord's choosing, without facing the caustic comments that I used to hear with reference to my partners growing weary of this "Christian crap" that allegedly undermined their own practices.

Others have been more polite, if not just as skeptical. Invariably my colleagues respond to my witness about the impact of Christian missions with comments like, "It's nice to finally be able to do what you want to do," or "I'm sure you're helping," though few if any are willing to acknowledge the source from which these seemingly destitute patients in the Third World derive their peace of mind—nor, for that matter, the source of my own.

That brings me to Dr. Robert Coles, yet another mentor from afar, who is a child psychiatrist and lecturer at Harvard University. He identified the crux of the problem in his Pulitzer Prize-winning five-volume series entitled *Children of Crisis*: "Rich kids who tried to break out of their sheltered surroundings and respond to the call of conscience [or God] presented a threat to others." At age 47, I too was a rich kid surrounded by rich peers. When my call came, apparently that was every bit as threatening for my colleagues as the thousands of children Coles interviewed for his work.[27]

Which brings to mind Jesus' Sermon on the Mount. The poor are mysteriously blessed with courage, peace of mind, and what Coles terms "a reservoir of inner strength." Compare that with the rich, who live in peril of the competition, quest for status, and fleeting financial gain that drives them. It is in this sense that Coles justifiably perceives wealth as a "distraction or impediment to what matters most." Using his life's view by way of contrast, Philip Yancey lays out his own indictment in inimitable fashion: "Good humanists work all their lives to improve the condition of the disadvantaged, but [without Christ] for what? To raise them to the level of the upper classes so that they too can experience boredom, alienation, and decadence?"[28]

With all due respect, that seems a little dogmatic to my way of thinking. Yet the same sort of unexpressed angst appears to apply to the academic community in my hometown—though here the threat is not so much to status and wealth as to "academic freedom," or lack thereof. Let me give you an example. A mutual friend in the history department at the local university attempted to arrange a debate between myself and a member of the so-called "Jesus Seminar" pertaining to the reliability of the four gospels and Acts as primary source materials on the life of Jesus. Two roadblocks, however, quickly emerged. For one, the chairman of the Department of Religious Studies where the debate was logically to be held feared controversy and, conceivably, "retribution, this being a state supported university"—or so it was lamely expressed to me. For another, my proposed opponent ultimately refused to debate someone like myself, who was "clearly an advocate" (rather than, I presume, an unbiased scholar like himself).

Now, as opposed to the track record of someone as esteemed as Robert Coles, my paltry credentials are such that no one need take notice. I understand that. What's more, Dr. Coles has the added distinction of being as meek as a sheep and as sly as a serpent, using the less obtrusive instrument of what he terms "spiritual literature" as a vehicle for his message at Harvard. As Coles so presciently observed: "That's how I carry the Bible tradition into the university, for it belongs there and it is a privilege to call upon it as a teacher."[29]

Why, then, do they invite Dr. Coles into what he ruefully acknowledges to be this "citadel of secular humanism?" To express it in his own self-deprecating if ever-penetrating way: "for idolatrous reasons...a name listed on a brochure." I appreciate where Dr. Coles is coming from; his credentials are impeccable. Yet it should not pass unnoticed that his spiritual transformation and subsequent Christian walk unfolded largely outside the constraints of the community in which he now resides. As for myself, peers both within the medical and academic communities have viewed my own about-face firsthand, and perceive it as a threat to those values the world compels them to embrace. So as not to fall victims to the same infection themselves, I have in a sense been "quarantined." That's the reality. Far from being a "prophet without honor" in his hometown,[30] however, I simply perceive myself as a donkey carrying the King's message to His people.

Perhaps the Lord allowed all of this to happen, because it was His way of reminding me that I was now doing God's work—not what I perceived to be my own. Rather than fulfilling a business contract for a fee, my new contract—no, covenant—is with Him on behalf of the lost sheep of His pasture. By declaring war on my practice, He nudged me toward greater commitment in the missions field abroad and among the poor here at home. This was, after all, what God had called me to do—what He had planned for me from the beginning—made as I was in His image.

That was a huge assignment, and required a character to match. Given the silver lining of privilege that had dissipated any storm clouds hovering over my first life, Jesus had every reason to question whether I was now up to the task. True, God will always take the time necessary to develop one's character to match the call. Yet therein lay the problem; I was already out in the missions field doing His work. My character needed maturing—and fast! He alone prompted me to recognize the situation for what it represented: I could fight as the secular world would do in the courts, or I could yield to the Lord as he reworked my life in preparation for His next, and bigger, assignment.

It was a painful yet profoundly valuable lesson. His purpose for me, as for all Believers, had been revealed in no uncertain terms: to do His will and complete His work. Each missions trip abroad confirms that lesson, with more cases, more effective witnessing, and better surgical results in the most difficult and challenging environments imaginable. All of which defies any explanation other than His presence in my life—not to mention in the clinics and operating rooms where He works beside me.

Jesus has given me no greater affirmation than this: that seeking *first* God's Kingdom and where He is at work is the key to both spiritual and professional fulfillment. The link that Professor Price, Dr. Coles, and I had been seeking all along—and which we all discovered in very different ways through our respective walks—has changed our lives immeasurably for the better. Not, most assuredly, because of anything we have done; rather, solely on account of the Lord's involvement. That's the righteousness He purchased in our behalf on the cross. That's what makes His promise a *reality* in the lives of every Believer, despite the persecution and spiritual warfare it necessarily entails.

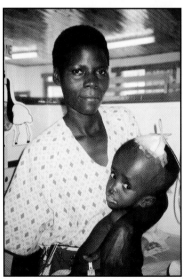

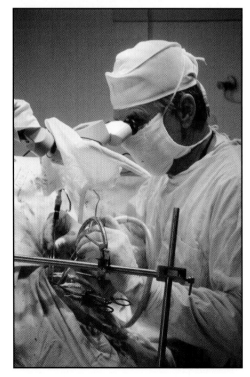

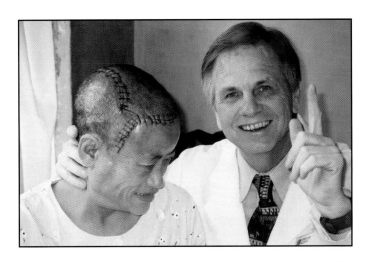

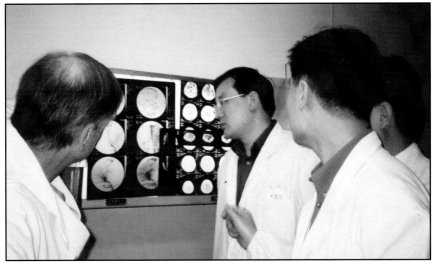

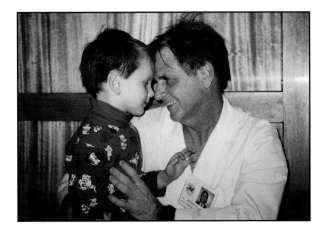

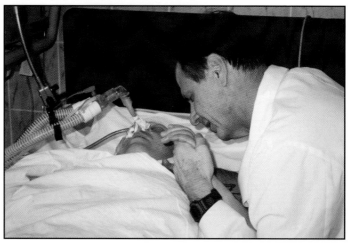

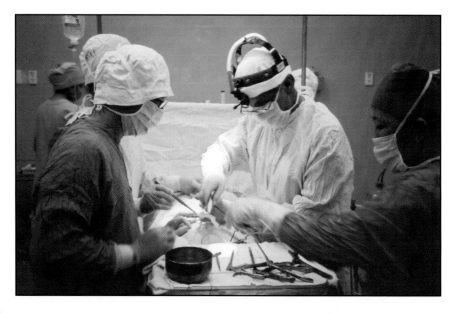

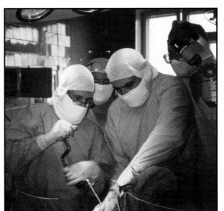

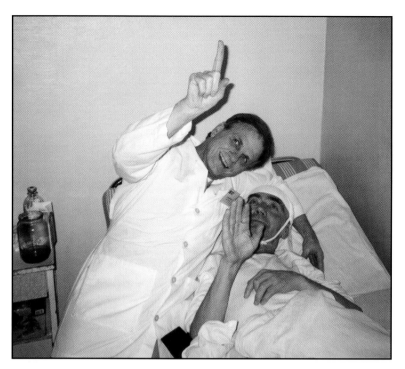

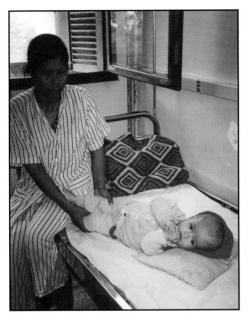

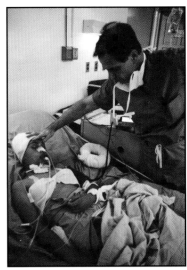

Salt and Light

It was tempting at this stage of my ministry to bypass the remaining Beatitudes in Matthew and turn to the last: "Blessed are you when people insult you, persecute you, and falsely say all manner of evil against you because of me. Rejoice and be glad, because great is your reward in heaven." Not only would that have been consistent with Luke's account, which ends there without addressing the remaining four blessings from the earlier gospel;[31] the good doctor immediately launches into a diatribe against the rich and well-positioned that admittedly reflected my own thinking at the time.[32] Yet God had no intention of puffing me up with self-righteousness. Lest I miss His point, He had given me Matthew's version of the Beatitudes to memorize, including the parables about salt and light appended to the conclusion. When viewed through these respective prisms, reality takes on a whole new meaning.

That is what two friends at different times and places taught me, when I was supposed to be witnessing to them. Not that Drs. Harry Torres or Le Ngoc Dung fancied themselves as teachers in a spiritual sense. As yet unaware of God's plan for their lives, they had more pressing matters to deal with—among them, unjustified persecution, which can be a bitter pill to swallow. After all, this comforting benediction to Jesus' Sermon on the Mount presupposes some foreknowledge of what He intends us to be in the body of Christ—whether salt that preserves His blessings, or light that reflects His love. Yet once my neurosurgical colleagues in Nicaragua and Vietnam, respectively, pondered their trials from these perspectives, God ultimately provided them some needed restitution. One regained his flavor; the other rekindled his flame. Both, to their credit, proved object lessons in humility. And both are parables for our times.

All of us are intimately familiar with that age-old adage, "Pride goes before a fall." We fail (and fall) often, I suppose, because we're just so good at it. As the root cause of sin, no doubt God is painfully aware of pride as well. That's why He sent His Son as a living sacrifice for our redemption. For those of us now poor enough in spirit to confess our transgressions, God has a way of picking fallen man up again—if not remaking us altogether.

I viewed one such recreation firsthand in Nicaragua, having been given the unusual privilege of both planting a seed and reaping the harvest there, albeit some four years in the making. During my first medical mission to Nicaragua in 1997, God introduced me to a neurosurgeon who epitomized the salt of the earth mentality as a self-made man—with all the excess baggage of pride that entailed. For many physicians, to be sure, this comes with the territory. Harry Torres was no exception. Not that his heart lacked compassion. That's what brought him back to his homeland from Canada to work among the poor at the Lenin Fonseca Hospital in Managua.

What Harry encountered upon his return was devastating. The economic heart of his once modestly prosperous country had been eviscerated by the recently deposed Sandinista regime. Revolutionary fervor and militant slogans the Sandinistas had; any realistic plans to build something out of the rubble they created never surfaced. Those few doctors, like Harry, that had chosen to return to Nicaragua labored under the constraints of its bankrupt medical system—as did their long-suffering patients, who bore their unaddressed concerns in silence.

Not so, my well-intentioned if occasionally bullheaded friend! Never one to tread softly in the face of injustice, Harry's stringent tongue alienated more often than it assuaged—particularly among his superiors. Eventually that got him into trouble. While I was there, the health-care crisis had accelerated to the point that the hospital's employees (including its physicians) arose from their stupor and declared a strike. Harry was there to lead the troops over the ramparts. Though they ultimately got a part of what their hospital and patients so desperately needed (including an increase in physician salaries from $100 to $300 a month!), the government predictably exacted revenge on their leaders. Harry was dismissed from the hospital and left to eke out a living for the next four years in the wasteland of "private practice," for which less than 5 percent of the population can afford to pay.

Throughout his exile in the wilderness, we kept in touch with e-mails and an occasional call. Continuing to witness to this paragon of pride, however, was no easy matter. Despite his own son being a missionary, Harry obstinately distrusted all organized religion; much less would he accept that he could ever become dependent on some mythical savior whose message was to turn the other cheek. Yet unbeknownst to my friend, God was surreptitiously working on his heart.

That became apparent three years later when I received an unexpected phone call. Harry was in Houston, Texas visiting his daughter, and insisted on driving up to visit me in Missouri. I chalked that up to his curiosity to see how the "other half" of his profession lived in America. Yet my friend had something far more important in mind.

The change in his countenance was remarkable. Harry's confident, can-do attitude had been replaced by a touch of humility and the softest of hearts. We talked long into the early morning hours about what he was going through. Eventually our conversation turned to those plans the Lord might have in store for this wounded warrior and his family. Having been through a similar circumstance of suffering professionally for what I believed in, we were kindred spirits. Far more important from God's perspective, Harry now understood in its most literal sense what that entailed.

Hence, his insistence on visiting me and attending church the following morning. That same evening my friends Mark and Mary Axness led Harry through the Sinner's Prayer, and he gave himself to the Lord.

Such a dramatic change in one who had been so self-reliant was a wonder for all to see—which, to Jesus' way of thinking, is precisely the point. How can salt regain the function for which it was intended? His Beatitudes offered my friend an answer: by surrendering to Him and serving as a preservative of all that is good and honorable. The implications for that in Nicaragua were huge. For a professional to use his occupation as a witness for Christ was like dropping a huge stone in a small pond, its ripple effect extending far beyond those secular shores that ostensibly defined Harry's workplace.

But would the salt retain its flavor once exposed to the harsh realities back home? I insisted on reciprocating his visit with a return to Nicaragua; after all, the apostle Paul had already alerted me to the potential problem: If God puts baby Christians under your care, that obligates you to stay with them until they reach spiritual maturity.[33] As a very poor imitation of Paul, I was now charged with nurturing the commitment of my new brother in Christ.

Knowing Harry Torres as I do, I should never have doubted him. Having sent my friend off with a Bible in Spanish and my favorite devotional, *Experiencing God*, he had continued to read avidly upon his return, and gained valuable insights into the Christian mindset—including his sheepish admission that he had never before understood what I had meant when signing off my e-mails with "In His name." One evening at dinner, with hands clasped in unity all around, Harry led the family through unaccustomed prayer, pouring out his heart to God. To be sure, he began self-consciously as if undergoing some trial by fire; by prayer's end, however, Harry positively glowed with the Christ-light. "Pass the salt," I envisioned him saying with a wink as he pointed to his heart. "This unleavened bread needs some seasoning!"

I wish that I could tell you that things have gotten better for his people; if anything, they were worse off than before. That was the second reason for my return to Nicaragua. The Ministry of Health was awash in red ink, broken instruments remained unrepaired, medications were unavailable, and the salt of the earth of Nicaragua continued to suffer accordingly. As for Harry, he was still out in the desert professionally. What's more, his former colleagues were threatening strike once again.

I felt as though I had never left the scene of a bleak tragicomedy. To quote an inimitable practitioner of the malapropism, "it was like déjà vu all over again"! With no realistic solutions in sight, my friends had come full circle without ever getting off the treadmill. At such pivotal times the salt either enhances what good remains, or is thrown out to be trampled underfoot. Some, like Harry, had already been discarded by those who held the purse strings as being allegedly spoiled and "no longer good for anything."[34] How shallow were such perceptions! His departure was their loss—and the Kingdom's gain. Nor was Harry as alone as he thought. In time, his colleagues at Lenin Fonseca would come to perceive themselves as grains of salt left to persevere in the Dead Sea of their moribund health-care system.

On the last evening I spent in Nicaragua, I came face to face with a recurring theme in the missions field: Jesus' ability to take a bad situation and make it better. To be metaphorically consistent, He has a way of reviving anything that seems hopelessly spoiled. Over a farewell dinner, I had the opportunity to share Christ with four of Harry's associates, among them the hospital's Chief Medical Officer and its Director. "How far could the ripple effect of Christ's ministry extend?" I wondered, and decided to put that to the test. Using a bowl of salt on the table as a makeshift hourglass, I challenged them to measure what they were going through from God's perspective.

Like Harry, they too may have felt they were being trampled underfoot—when what they had really been given was an opportunity to build up treasures in heaven. "When you do this to the least of these," Christ had said, "you do it unto me." For the first time in their own wilderness, my friends caught a glimpse of what it means to be a truly dependent servant. As grains of salt being painfully sifted through the hourglass of such a withering environment, they were preservatives as much as markers of time—God's time, to be precise. It was a sacred moment. Through His grace, hearts were being transformed before my very eyes.

I left Nicaragua the following morning convinced beyond a shadow of doubt that the seed God had planted four years before in one of their own would take root in Harry's former colleagues. Not through anything he or I had done; rather, the Christ-light had been reflected through a cracked vessel of salt that evening, and its afterglow still lingers. Of that I am certain. Through His divine plan, hearts are changing among physicians there, now recognizing, as they do, the eternal inheritance to be gained by running the race as servants to a higher call.

Such grace—and its eternal rewards—only He can provide. Which is another way of reminding ourselves that we labor under the constraints of God's timeline, not our own. Once we accept that, such admonitions as "pride goes before a fall" become sacred blessings. As one of my friends so beautifully put it at the end of the evening: "Pride falls before a gracious God."

⚬━✦━⚬

Not that pride is always the problem. When the most humble of souls is steamrolled by forces beyond his or her control, that's even more of an affront to God. Le Ngoc Dung is a case in point, with whom I had the privilege of working in South Vietnam. There, the poverty of the medical system is superseded only by the poverty of spirit engendered by living under an oppressive communist regime. Yet darkness cannot abide the light, and in a poor provincial hospital in Danang, a flame still lingers in the heart of its Vice-director and Chief of Neurosurgery. Naturally, I assumed that one so well positioned had the necessary clout to act as a mover and shaker for his people. Yet appearances were deceiving. Le's past involvement in the Vietnam war dictated otherwise. That my friend still practices neurosurgery at all is something of a miracle. Let me explain.

As a medical officer in the South Vietnamese army during the war, Le had been trained by two American neurosurgeons at the air-base in Danang. When the country was overrun by the communist advance in 1975, virtually all of his colleagues fled the city for points south and beyond. Le, however, stayed on; indeed, he never considered doing anything else. "These were my people," he later explained with a resigned shrug of his shoulders, "and I was their doctor."

That noble gesture was rewarded with three years in a "reeducation facility," the communist euphemism for a concentration camp. To make matters worse, the country's leading neurosurgeon was charged with the unenviable task of defusing land mines during his internment! The only thing that rescued Le from professional purgatory and almost certain death was the fact that he had treated many Vietcong prisoners during the war, some of whom were highly placed officers. Once they became aware of their former surgeon's perilous plight, they petitioned the powers that be for his release.

Never one to rock the boat, Le quietly returned to his practice among the people he loved in Danang, and gradually worked his way up the medical hierarchy. Not that he would—or could—ever reach the top in such a politically controlled system. Drawing upon our own civil war as an analogy, Le reminded me that former Confederate leaders may have been reincorporated into the establishment, but were never given top positions of authority. That hardly mattered to my friend anyway; in his self-effacing manner, he acknowledged that "he was an Indian, not a chief," who simply desired to serve his people with the skills he had been given.

Le in fact views his current mandated position in the political establishment as the supreme irony: he is the designated director of Vietnam's repatriation program, charged with convincing those who fled the country during the war to return to the homeland with inducements of jobs and free housing. Is he bitter? No—and for a decidedly heretical reason by communist standards. Having been educated as a youth by French-speaking Catholics, my gentle friend has somehow managed to retain a measure of God's grace and forgiveness.

Intimations of that were spelled out on his office chalkboard just above a reminder of the date of my arrival. It was a quote from the scientist-turned-Christian advocate Blaise Pascal that read: "We are not to behave as animals, but to pursue the virtues of love and knowledge." Peering into the eyes of this soft-spoken saint, as he introduced himself and grasped my hand with both his own, told me all I needed to know. That hardly prepared me, however, for what this official in the communist hierarchy then said with characteristic humility: "I believe it is God who sent you here."

Despite the most restrictive circumstances imaginable, in all my travels I have never so quickly developed such abiding friendship and love for one of my own profession. That's not to mention the risks for himself in harboring the same feelings. My own boldness as a Christian witness accelerated accordingly. I immediately dubbed him "Lighthouse," and reinforced his new identity thereafter with daily verses of Scripture concerning Jesus being a light to the nations—and, by extension, Le being a light to his people.

Little did I know that my chosen metaphor was so appropriate. Le had envisioned all along that his neurosurgery department in Danang would someday become a "center of excellence," situated as it was in the center of the country where the poor could not afford to travel to the more cosmopolitan centers of Hanoi to the north and Ho Chi Min City to the south. His vision gave me ample justification to introduce Christ's Beatitudes, pointing out to my friend that, as a "light to [his] world, a city on a hill cannot be hidden. Neither do people light a lamp and put it under a bowl. Instead, they put it on a stand, and it gives light to the entire house."[35] Nodding in affirmation as Le read this passage, I thought I detected a tear in his eye once his own mandate leaped from the page: "In the same way, let your light shine before men, that they might see your good deeds and praise your Father in heaven."[36]

Nor was it any accident that God reciprocated by leading the two of us through several difficult tumor resections and microvascular decompressions during our weeks of sharing. The good results spoke for themselves, and Le had no difficulty making the implied connection: anything done in the Lord's name is a witness for Him. Before I left Danang, my friend would reciprocate in kind by giving me a small lamp with a candle as a going-away gift, reminding me to light it at Christmas in honor of our friendship and He who had made that possible.

Viewed through the prism of the Christ-light, Pascal's quote became a bridge that linked two neurosurgeons from very different cultures as kindred spirits. Not only had Le alerted me in a less than subtle fashion that his heart had at some point been touched by God; this bridge, fashioned of science and literature, alerted us both to the fact that ours indeed was a divine appointment.

That hardly dispelled altogether the adversity and disappointments we shared during my first visit. For one, the customs officials refused to release our medical team's shipment of supplies, including an operating microscope that I was to donate to the hospital. Yet God will not be mocked! Perhaps He was telling the Vietnamese authorities as much by unleashing three consecutive nights of thunderous storms that knocked out the electricity in the entire city—the lone exception being the fifth floor conference room of the hotel where our team stood in intercessory prayer for the people now shrouded in darkness. It did not pass unnoticed among those praying that the communist party building two blocks to the west was not only pitch black, but was dwarfed by the structure where we were staying, its top floor inexplicably bathed in light. Does God *really* speak through nature? Make of this what you will, but of *His* will there could be no doubt during the first three days before customs finally relented and approved the shipment's release: "You are the light of the world. [Even a dimly lit hotel] on a hill cannot be hidden."

Though the authorities never released the microscope, there remains a silver lining in the storm clouds that enveloped Danang that fateful week. To bring the scope to God's intended place will require my returning to Vietnam a third time to deliver it personally. This is His way of assuring that our relationship will be rekindled despite what stumbling blocks any worldly principality throws in our path. Yet, once again, we are charged with working on God's timeline, not our own. And Le understands that as well. Accordingly, this very gentle soul, along with his suffering people, will wait patiently as that timeline is played out.

No, darkness cannot abide the light—and in this port city where America first became irrevocably involved in Vietnam when the marines waded ashore there in 1965, a beacon still shines to cut through bureaucratic oppression and dashed hopes. The Kafkaesque nightmare of our long day's journey into night in Southeast Asia is being dispelled by the Christ-light, of which one long-suffering Vietnamese neurosurgeon is an abiding reflection. Under the Lord's aegis, Americans are finally returning to Vietnam to finish a conflict that never really ended—yet on this occasion, a conflict of eternal consequences fought by Christian soldiers bearing not M-16s, but John 3:16.

Second Witness

They Will Be Shown Mercy

If one theme typified my experience in Siberia, it is that things in this dark recess of the world are never quite what they seem. To His credit, for which I am eternally grateful, Jesus had a great deal to do with that while we were there—what with His unanticipated healing of the lady with a stroke in an equally improbable apartment-setting shortly after our arrival in Bradsk. That I had arrived *at all* was something of a miracle in itself, attributable only to the mercy the Lord extends to the merciful as promised in His fifth Beatitude. Presumably He makes allowances on occasion for the foolish as well; for the very night we were to leave Krasnyorsk, I managed to fulfill both criteria by misplacing my passport.

Needless to say, that was no small matter in the eyes of the Russian authorities. One of the other team members had already been detained for having entered the country with an expired passport, and spent the next three days in the airport waiting for the embassy to free him from house arrest. The fact that the Gulag was only a stone's throw away now added a touch of drama to my own predicament. To make matters more unnerving still, I had volunteered to travel to Bradsk on a chartered Russian cargo plane with three others who, like myself, had been asked to stay behind in Krasnyorsk to deal with some political fall-out that had arisen there in the press. We were scheduled to leave in an hour, at which point a lost passport was certain to be of interest to the priggish airport security.

A heavily guarded doorway separated me from the cargo plane sitting on the tarmac outside. Enter Jesus and my three brothers, who came to the rescue. Embracing me in a prayer circle with laying on of hands, they anointed my forehead with oil. That may have seemed little more than a ritualistic gesture—until the time came to board the plane. Inexplicably, my passport (or lack of it) was not checked as I went through the security gate. It was as if Paul and Silas had found their jail cell mercifully open after spending all evening in prayer and simply walked to freedom, bringing their jailer to Christ in the process. The last, sad to relate, I didn't take the liberty of doing. Not that this made the open tarmac laying before me any less of an affirmation in my own eyes....

As so often happens after experiencing such a spiritual high, I should have steeled myself to go back down into the valley. Nothing had prepared me for the journey I was about to take on the rickety cargo plane piloted by two less than sober Russians, who just happened to have a stash of Vodka in the cockpit! That I was being taken up in the air and not down in the valley offered no more comfort than the "seating" arrangements. We were relegated to the tail section, jam-packed with medical supplies. To our dismay, not only was the plane not pressurized, it also had no heat. I sprawled out on an Action Packer, enshrouded in nylon webbing like a hapless fly caught in a spider web, acutely attuned to any changes in the engine's vibration that might herald impending disaster. There being no windows in the tail, we had no way of orienting ourselves. The only indications that our plane was taking off, and eventually landing, were the painful pressure changes during the ascent and descent.

For two interminable hours we clung to the netting with hands numbed by the bitter cold, the roar of the engines deafening us, and the stench of diesel fuel filling the air. More prayers were said during what we perceived as an "ascent" into hell than during the rest of the mission combined! I sensed intuitively how a drug smuggler must feel—wedged between cargo boxes, his heart in his throat, and his passport in absentia. Yet God had plans for the four of us in Bradsk, and we lived to tell the tale.[37]

⚬═══╪═══⚬

As one other measure of His mercy shown the merciful, our arrival there coincided with a huge neurosurgical triumph on the Lord's behalf—something that only He made possible by compelling me to take some specialized spinal instrumentation along. Though I originally intended to use this equipment for teaching purposes, Jesus had something more important in mind. That became apparent during our first day on rounds in the Bradsk hospital. I was asked to consult on a middle-aged lady who had suffered a severe fracture-dislocation of her cervical spine with resultant quadriplegia. She had been bedridden for three months, waiting to die of pneumonia or a pulmonary embolism that the majority of such patients eventually suffer. Her MRI scan revealed one of the most devastating injuries I can recall ever seeing: the sixth vertebra had been so dislodged that it sat in *front* of the seventh, with no remaining canal available through which the spinal cord could pass.

Her diagnosis was in keeping with my perception that things are never quite what they seem in Siberia. It had probably been weeks since anyone had done a neurological examination on this all but abandoned soul. What I found on my own was a huge surprise: she had some retained sensation in her left foot and was able to detect applied pressure to both legs. Though unable to move any of her extremities voluntarily, these meager findings at least indicated that some neurologic function inexplicably remained. Not wishing to embarrass my Russian colleagues with these "new" findings, I reviewed the MRI scan on my own again after rounds. A single view suggested that, perhaps, the spinal cord was not transected after all.

Insofar as the dislocated vertebrae had already all but fused, this was small consolation. That said, the doctors in Bradsk had been unable to mobilize this poor lady even in a wheelchair due to

79

the intense pain from her grotesque and unstable deformity. If for no other possible gain than to get her out of bed and perhaps forestall the inevitable, I volunteered to operate in hopes of reducing the fracture and stabilizing it with the titanium plate and screws the Lord had thrown in my bag at the last moment. Without an operating microscope, a power drill, or even traction to reduce the injury, however, that would be a formidable and (at least by traditional neurosurgical standards) foolish undertaking.

Yet not by God's; He always makes a way if that fits into His plans. Despite the overwhelming odds against completing the operation, He led me safely through it in full view of a host of skeptical Russian nurses and doctors literally looking over my shoulder. At the close of the procedure we had a nice looking Xray with a realigned spine secured by the only plate I had brought. What's more, it just happened to have been the precise size required. Another one of those amazing coincidences, I'm sure....

Such a "minor" manifestation of His mercy to me hardly compared with what the Lord had in store for everyone the following morning. Inquiring on rounds as to how my patient was feeling, she broke into a huge, toothless grin, gave me "two thumbs up" (literally) with hands that had been lifeless the day before, and then proceeded to raise both of her legs off the bed! Here, but for the grace of God, was an otherwise totally inexplicable reversal of fortune in the face of an "irreversible" injury—in, of all places, Siberia. She would walk again!

I fell on my knees in thanksgiving, numbly reciting over and over the one verse that seemed so applicable for the moment: "Blessed are the merciful, for they shall be shown mercy." Through no merit of our own, Jesus had clearly bequeathed this to servant and sufferer alike. What had seemed a fruitless undertaking on my part, He had blessed. As for my patient, the Lord had chosen through His mercy to acknowledge yet another paralytic's suffering and answer it with a command: "Take up your mat and walk!" Never have I been so filled with awe in the presence of His healing power than at that moment—not to mention astounded by the timeless truth of His Word, which the Beatitudes once again had confirmed.

My Russian colleagues, of course, simply acknowledged this miracle as little more than a show of Yankee ingenuity blessed with some technology that they did not have. Though hardly surprised by their reaction, I knew better. This was *His* doing, not mine. Time after time the Lord had made it abundantly clear to his disciples that miracles don't lead to lasting faith; rather, faith only affirms the miraculous. Shortly thereafter, He would remind me of that elemental truth through the faith of the nurse that accompanied us to the apartment of the elderly woman who had suffered a stroke. Unlike the neurosurgeon who had assisted me in the spinal operation earlier that week, she could not be dissuaded that a miracle was in the works on this occasion without surgery. And the truth of the matter is, both miracles merely affirmed God's ability to suspend the laws of probability if it served His purpose.

⚬━━✦━━⚬

Nothing prepared me, however, for how such abiding faith can transform lives despite physical healing not being in the cards. The last night before leaving Siberia for home, I made my final housecall, still reeling from the miracle I had witnessed two days before. An articulate, well-dressed lady had visited the clinic, asking specifically for a neurosurgeon who might visit her friend. She explained that two years before, an intruder had broken into the friend's home, murdered her husband, and stabbed her in the neck, rendering her immediately paralyzed from the shoulders down. The obvious fact that there was little I could do for her medically now was immaterial; drawn by the pathos of this tragic story, I and three others agreed to go to her apartment that evening.

There we found Ludmilla surrounded by three friends plus the lady I had met in the clinic, all of whom had taken turns tending to her needs in shifts, twenty-four hours a day, seven days a week. Their steadfast faith conjured up visions of the paralytic described in the fifth chapter of Luke,[38] who had been brought by four companions to Jesus to be healed. Finding the doorway too crowded to enter, they had climbed up on the roof, cut a hole in it, and lowered their charge down to a startled Jesus below. The parallels were so striking that I immediately opened my Bible and read the account to them through our interpreter. What bore emphasizing was Jesus' comment that it was because of the faith of the *stretcher-bearers* that their friend's sins would be forgiven and his paralysis healed. Now, two thousand years later, we stood face to face with four like-minded Carers of whom the Lord had spoken....

That was the bridge we used to cross over into a discussion about Jesus. Proudly nodding to an icon sitting on the mantle, Ludmilla affirmed that she "knew something about God," but could not worship Him unless she was able to go to church. Dumbfounded, I responded by picking up my guitar and singing a song that seemed so aptly titled for the moment: "Surely the Presence of the Lord Is in This Place." Though no one in the room doubted that, Ludmilla still seemed perplexed. She confessed that she felt His presence, but didn't know how to communicate with Him.

Taken aback, I responded: "Well, you pray."

"I'm willing," she replied. "I know I cannot be healed, but to have my sins forgiven is more than I deserve. How, then, do you pray?" Oh, how the Lord opens doors! Immediately I turned a few pages further to Luke chapter 11 where one of Jesus' disciples had asked in all earnestness, "Lord, teach us to pray." We then read together word for word what Jesus instructed His disciples to pray: the Lord's Prayer....

That evening, four merciful stretcher-bearers and a paralytic came to the Lord, each spoken to across the barriers of language through the timeless truth of His Word they had waited a seeming lifetime to hear: "Blessed are the merciful, for they shall be shown mercy." As for myself, that was simply a manifestation of God's grace. Jesus had prepared me for just such a moment when, as a neurosurgeon, I had nothing to bring to the table. Certainly He had not chosen the gifted, for I had no gifts of my own to offer. Rather, He had gifted the chosen with the Good News. Through us—not because of us— the Lord had made a way when there seemed to be no way.

They Will See God

If ever I needed affirmation in what I thought God had called me to do, it had been during my first trip to El Salvador. Having turned tail on the values of my former life, and acutely aware of the problems that had created for me back home, Eric's tragedy had been a sobering introduction to the mission field. Though Jesus clearly had shouldered my burden down in this dark valley, I was having trouble seeing the Christ-light that His sixth Beatitude had promised. "Pure in heart"? I'd like to think so. Troubled in mind? You bet! Such self-absorption prevented me from "seeing God" and focusing on His plans for my new life.

That is but one reason the Lord had brought an angel unaware to the clinic outside San Salvador on the final day of the most trying week imaginable—to affirm once again why I had been called there in the first place. The other reason had more important and far-reaching consequences: though the sixth Beatitude proclaims that the pure in heart are blessed because they shall see God, some assistance on their behalf is occasionally required—like a $2.00 pair of reading glasses. Let me explain.

For several days I had noticed an elderly peasant woman waiting patiently in the rear of the line. Somehow she always managed to "miss the cut" at the end of the day, and would find herself back where she started on the next. Eventually I lost track of this paragon of patience—only to see her return on the final day of the clinic shortly after we had closed and were packing up our gear. Through an interpreter, her daughter explained that she had come for an eye examination.

This had been a pervasive request throughout the two weeks; everyone, it seemed, wanted glasses. The ophthalmologists had been so overwhelmed with requests for refractions that a huge backlog there prevented many patients from being seen. My solution for the problem was simple: rather than wait for a formal eye examination, I commandeered a hundred or so pairs of reading glasses from the ophthalmology storeroom. Thereafter, whenever someone asked to see an eye doctor, I simply took three of them from my knapsack and had the patient try them on in labeled sequence—"weak," "medium," and "strong." Once their faces lit up, that was all we needed: diagnosis and treatment in one fell swoop! What's more, the eye clinic lines were reduced considerably.

Yet that was then; this was today. The little lady was inconsolable in her grief once she discovered that the eye clinic was closed and all of our glasses had already been packed on board the bus waiting to take us to the airport. I frantically dug into my knapsack to see if I had any left. At the very bottom I found one pair labeled "strong." She tried them on—and immediately broke into a huge grin. Fumbling in her coat pocket, she then pulled out a dog-eared copy of the Gospel of John and began reading out loud. Tears of joy streamed down her face as I stood there with a perplexed look on my own.

After all, such a profoundly emotional response seemed out of keeping with the quiet stoicism she had manifested throughout the week, and I mentioned that to her daughter. "But you don't understand," she replied. "There are fourteen members of our extended family, all of whom found the Lord through my mother." And as it turned out, she had been the spiritual head not only of her own household, but for many of the neighbors as well. Yet then, rather precipitately, her eyes began to fail ten years ago, and she could no longer read to them from His Word. "This is the first time she's been able to see print since the onset of her blindness," her daughter informed me. "The Bible is her bread of life. Please forgive her for overreacting. She's been very hungry; and so have we. You see, no one else in our family can read."

Forgive her? Awestruck silence in the presence of a saint was all that I could muster! Here was the spiritual head of the family, the purest of hearts, whose lamp had been snuffed out for a decade— with all that portended for the famished sheep of her pasture. A $2.00 pair of reading glasses was the only thing that had kept her from "seeing" God— and others to see Him through her eyes. This affirmed in bold print why I had been the last doctor to board the bus, and why He saw to it that I had not given all of my glasses away. "Blessed are the pure in heart, for they shall see God." Granted. Yet sometimes we have the privilege of helping those with hearts far purer than our own to find their way in the darkness.

<hr />

On the rarest of occasions the servant is given the opportunity to be a conduit of light in a more sanctified setting, as the Lord did for me one evening in Argentina. That's when He took me to a higher level of unearned reward at a revival attended by some two hundred new converts to Christ, whom we had treated in the clinic that day. There had been an altar call at the end of the service, and the pastor graciously invited members of the medical team to come down to the front to share in our patients' declaration for the Lord. As we mingled among the crowd of newly-born Believers gathered at the altar in prayer, I instinctively laid my hand on the head of one elderly farmer, who was trembling and sobbing, in an effort to comfort him.

Others apparently saw my gesture differently. The moment I touched the man, his eyes rolled back and he fell into the arms of his son, who gently lowered him to the ground. Immediately I felt the tug on my sleeve from a little girl, who beckoned me to come over and "bless" her mother in like fashion. The same thing happened! In quick succession others gently guided me to their friends or loved ones. I began to pray with each, then laid hands upon them while others gathered behind in anticipation of the "fall." And so it continued, one right after another, as the Lord accompanied me on the most humbling spiritual journey I have ever had the privilege to take. It was His way of leading me, if only for the moment, to a higher level of affirmation by allowing me to *see* what He had been to the sheep of His flock for two millennia.

Imagine! An unordained layman with no other credentials than a heart for the Lord, who had been granted the privilege of wearing His robes as a minister rather than the physician I was. As the praying continued, the ground around us became littered with bodies in various stages of spiritual repose. It was as if a great battle was being waged here, and the "casualties" were growing with each passing minute. A battle-ground? Yes, for men's souls…. And Jesus was the victor, with whom I was standing (by grace alone) in His hour of triumph. For the Lord knew my heart—and though by no means as pure as originally conceived in His mind's eye, I had been called into my Creator's presence to share in the vision He had for mankind from the beginning. Blessed at that moment were we all; for we had truly *seen* God, just as He had promised.

As the youth praise-and-worship team continued to play up on the stage, I marveled over the countless ways Christ gives us our affirmation. This presupposes, of course, that we recognize and accept what our own spiritual gift is—and mine, most assuredly, was not as a song leader. Why, just that very morning, I had brought my guitar to our devotional and led the group through a smattering of hymns that I had learned. Though my motives had been as pure as my love for the Lord in so doing, that certainly had not come across as a spiritual gift—an admission I'm forced to make each time I rekindle the fantasy of serving in that capacity. After removing His earplugs(!), Jesus gently reprimanded me in His own inimitable fashion: "Bert, why don't you leave the music to others and use the gift of compassion I gave to you? I think you'll like the fit, because *My* heart is what I want others to see in you." That wasn't what I had envisioned when I joined Him at the altar; yet it was enough for others to witness on this sacred evening in a rural village in Argentina. Which is why the pure in heart are so blessed: they *see* God in our service to them.

They Will Be Called Sons of God

Sometimes, despite good intentions and even the Lord's blessing, the bridge of reconciling others to Christ simply cannot be crossed. The people to whom the missionary witnesses may be so unreachable, callous, or just plain *lost*—and the cultural/political milieu in which he or she labors so oppressive—that it's difficult to reconcile the effort being expended on their behalf, much less reconcile them to God. It's at this point the Lord reminds us that what we've been called to do is for Him—and in a time and place of His choosing. Jesus alone is the Great Reconciler. Only He knows which hearts can be changed.

That's why the Lamb of God came into this fallen world to begin with—as a peacemaker. The missionary merely carries His message to the destitute and devious alike. Yet only to the extent to which we *ourselves* are at peace with the Son determines how successful we are on His Father's behalf. Which is what I believe Jesus meant when He told His disciples: "My peace I give to you. I do not give as the world gives."[39]

Nor as the world receives; hence the difficulty of witnessing in communist countries today. The Gospel is hardly welcome—much less received—by the leadership of such "secular principalities" as North Korea, Cuba, China, and Vietnam. As regards medical missions in particular, what their Ministers of Health give and receive is "as the world gives" (and receives). Any justification for your being there despite pure and unselfish motives is weighed practically by their own.

Communism remains the state "religion," and the depth of the people's commitment to that is in direct proportion to the control of their minds. The gifts their leaders receive gladly. The message is merely tolerated—and that only *pro forma* at the negotiating table before entering the country, not once you're out on the street or seeing patients in the clinic—despite the Lord's abiding presence there.

To my chagrin, I had ignored that reality after leaving North Vietnam following what initially promised to be a literal harvest on behalf of God's children there. Two of us had been invited to work with a surgeon at the National Pediatric Institute in Hanoi. What made that joint venture so gratifying for my companion, Ron, a Vietnam war veteran, was not only the obvious fact that both he and the North Vietnamese surgeon had fought on opposite sides of the conflict; they had faced *each other* on the same battlefield near the Demilitarized Zone! To have the privilege of sharing in the healing of her children thirty years later represented peacemaking of the highest order. Despite the Lord's blessing of exorcising demons from the past, however, Jesus' promise that we might be acknowledged as "Sons of God" by those we served was not to be.

Far from it in the end; that sobering edict was handed down from somewhere above. We're not referring to heaven here, but to an entrenched oligarchy hunkered down in paranoia—less so against the United States than the real Kingdom we represented. Their "rice-bowl mentality"[40] was not sufficient to assuage such paranoia, despite the gifts we had to confer. I had arranged to return to Hanoi the next year and donate an operating microscope to the Institute. In this day and age, microsurgical techniques are considered essential for achieving satisfactory results in the removal of brain tumors and the like—particularly in the pediatric population. Though her children would have benefited immensely (as there are no operating microscopes in all of North Vietnam), the invitation to return to Hanoi never surfaced.

Peacemakers? Most assuredly; even the rigid Vietnamese leadership was willing to acknowledge that. Yet "Sons of God"? Not in their eyes! The silence from Hanoi to this day remains deafening—a harsh reminder that though the Lord may open doors, there will always be men to close them.[41]

○━✦━○

China is another case in point; yet even there the system cannot sweep Christ's legacy under the rug altogether. Let me give you an example. Speaking one evening at dinner with a former army officer who had taken a job in the bureaucracy as Director of the Handicapped Association in Wuhan, I realized that even the most hardened of hearts had softened in spite of itself by caring for these unfortunate wards of the state. No doubt this man was willing to indulge my witness (if only temporarily) simply to reap the practical benefits. Yet a single offhanded comment he made that evening spoke volumes to my suspicion that the Divine Reconciler, unbeknownst to him, was working on his heart. "There's something in what you Christians have to say," he conceded. Considering the source, that was an astounding admission!

In one sense, however, his comment had not come as a complete surprise. An elderly man whom I had met on the street the day before (dressed in characteristic Maoist garb of his generation) unconsciously betrayed how such sentiments could occasionally surface, even in one of the most mind-controlling regimes. Recognizing me to be an American, he had asked me three things: how old I was, what I did for a living, and was I a Christian? The last question caught me off guard, and I later asked an expatriate who taught English in the school system there to explain what the old Maoist had meant. She told me that such a question is often asked of Americans, and for one reason. Throughout the twentieth century that had begun with the distasteful intrusion of foreigners across China's closed borders, its people had learned through harsh experience that the only "good" foreigners were Christians. All others had their own agendas.

Therein lay the seed of God's Kingdom here on earth, one that had been planted in the rockiest of soils overgrown with thistles of autocracy. Yet it was a seed nonetheless; and it had survived despite no conscious attempts on their own behalf to cultivate it. In just such subtle ways the roots of the Gospel are making inroads into the most hostile environments, one heart at a time: an aging Maoist on the one hand; a middle-aged bureaucrat on the other—the one subconsciously monitoring the Lord's work; the other unwittingly laboring in His field.

Many of China's younger professionals, to be sure, want to labor in a place of their own choosing—and are willing to put their trust in God to make that happen. Just ask Dr. Zhang Wen Ben, an admitted agnostic, with whom I had worked in Xi'an City. This gifted doctor had passed a very stringent examination in order to further his training at an esteemed neurosurgical hospital in Beijing. Only 10 percent of such candidates pass; despite such an exemplary performance, a recent e-mail I received from Zhang assured me that oppression is alive and well in China. As my friend ruefully acknowledged: "I've wanted to tell you for some time that I passed the doctoral examination, but as soon as I knew the results, the director of our hospital told me they would not let me study in Beijing. He simply said 'we agreed for you to take the examination, but we are not sure we agreed for you to study elsewhere if you passed.'"

Zhang was thrown into a severe depression, and is considering resigning from his hospital. In the Chinese medical system, that would be tantamount to committing professional suicide. Yet what followed in his e-mail was affirmation of the highest sort that, just perhaps, my witness to this former skeptic had not been in vain. Having surreptitiously slipped him a Bible before I left, Zhang had apparently taken Moses' "Let my people go" appeal to heart. "This is very important to me as you must know, but is a situation I don't want to face," he admitted. "Therefore, *let us pray to God together*" (emphasis mine). Staring at this poignant plea on my computer screen, I was suddenly overcome and fell to my knees—as much with thanksgiving as for intercession.

As for China's youngest generation, a pervasive, if subliminal message threatens the prevailing mind-set altogether: Jesus' familiar refrain, "Let the children come." For it's through the plight of her handicapped children (their poor in spirit) that the Lord's door has been wedged open in more than one strategically placed heart I encountered there. And that's enough to sustain the missionary in the tomb-like confines of oppression that typify China today. Never underestimate the power of the Holy Spirit. When used as a wedge, it can roll even the largest stone away....

⊶────⊷

"Blessed are the peacemakers," Jesus assured us, "for they shall be called Sons of God." No doubt that is true in His Kingdom, but not necessarily in mother Russia. Any act of kindness done there on humanitarian grounds—and then judged by them—is as fleeting as the writer of Ecclesiastes had warned us it would be: "I have seen all things that are alone under the sun: all of them are meaningless as chasing after the wind.... Vanity, all is vanity."

Our team learned this painful lesson firsthand on the day we were to leave for Bradsk. To our detriment, we had been allied with the wrong wing of the political spectrum from the moment we set foot on the frozen tundra of Siberia. If the truth be known, our Russian sponsor had in mind a humanitarian gesture that would fulfill his own aspirations—carving a niche for himself in the field of presidential candidates angling for the post shortly to be vacated by the ailing Boris Yeltsen. From this Jewish entrepreneur's perspective (whose keys our Christian organization had shamelessly used to open the Kremlin door), this particular mission was nothing more than a down payment on his campaign promises.

Accordingly, the public perception of what we had accomplished was grossly distorted by the press, which happened to be controlled by the opposing political party. We were dumbfounded to learn through an interpreter that the media had cast our mission's accomplishments in a very dim light. The headlines told the tale: our "heart team" had lost four patients, and one of my own aneurysm patients had died. Though both claims were untrue, that

91

wasn't the half of it: we didn't even have a heart team doing operations in Krasnyorsk!

No matter. As seems to be typical of the media everywhere, they were more intent upon making the news than reporting it. I was promised an opportunity by the hospital administrator where we had worked to set the record straight at a press conference that afternoon, while the remainder of the team flew on to Bradsk. As befits the political chicanery that typifies virtually everything Russian, however, the press conference never materialized.

⊶—✦—⊷

Nowhere is that harsh indictment more applicable than in Russia's antiquated medical system, if the pervasive influence of the Mafia (and the lack of influence in those that govern) is any indication. Among the system's many harsh realities is the inability to capitalize on the skills of its health-care workers, because of the chronic shortage of medical equipment. That's probably the only reason I had been invited to work with a team of five neurosurgeons and a neuroradiologist in the regional medical center of Krasnyorsk—provided I would bring with me the necessary surgical and radiology supplies to treat an astounding backlog of patients with aneurysms, brain tumors, hydrocephalus, and the like. Though the work was some of the most gratifying, if challenging, surgery I have had the privilege to undertake abroad, my Russian friends simply were not open to what I had to tell them of Jesus. The neuroradiologist who doubled as my translator underscored the point: "We're just trying to make it day by day, and don't have the luxury of thinking about spiritual matters. After all, God doesn't put bread in my children's mouths."

His comment struck me as ironic, if not altogether sad. When political, economic, or social circumstances leave people nowhere else to turn, faith in God often flourishes to fill the void.[42] That's but one of many black holes in the former Soviet Union casting a lingering shadow over its people: three-quarters of a century's worth, to be exact. During the communist era, not only the Russian Orthodox Church, but all religion, fell into disfavor. For all intents and purposes, fully two generations of Russians have never known God.

This may also explain, in part, the impenetrable darkness enveloping Russia's floundering capitalist experiment, paradoxically governed by the black market, where only the "fit" (read: selfish) survive. As for her "government-controlled" hospitals, doctors close up shop and leave at mid-afternoon to tend to their vegetable gardens at home—not as a hobby, but as a necessity; otherwise, there is nothing but bread and coarse mutton for their families to eat.

Nor do their patients wait for the doctors' return with any particular sense of urgency; they're already accustomed to waiting, as the system cannot begin to supply their needs. Any medical supplies that are budgeted for in January are depleted by March. Should a patient have an aneurysm that requires clipping, that had better happen within the first three months of the year; otherwise there are no clips left to do the surgery! The fateful alternative is an inevitable rebleed leading to stroke or death.

Russia's women fare even worse, victims of what is caustically referred to as the "Illness of Perestroika." Alcoholism has reached epidemic proportions among females there today. Dispossessed by the system in every sense of the word, prostitution has become the only way for many to survive. Any pain, guilt, or loneliness this may engender is assuaged with vodka. What's more, the Russian preoccupation with sex and pornography that sustains this cancer is fed by x-rated films, the only available TV programming (at least in the two hotels where our team stayed).

One evening I asked my interpreter, Sasha, whether he preferred the new system or the old before the fall of communism in 1990. His answer came as a shock, and spoke to the spiritual emptiness that grips the former Soviet Union. "As a child [in the old system], I had a greater sense of security and hope for the future than I do now. Though we can only dream of what capitalism might someday afford, we miss the political stability that communism at one time gave us." He then conjured up an old Russian saying to make his point, whether applied to the impotent leadership that rules in name only, or the Mafia that really greases the wheel: "It's always the head of the fish that stinks first." These were harsh (and ironic) words for myself, a Christian missionary, who had cut my spiritual teeth on the assumption that I had been chosen to be "a fisher of men." Unintentionally, Sasha was ripping huge holes in my net. No matter which side of the boat I cast it, the catch seemed so despoiled that I had to sublimate the temptation to stay safely in port.

"Orphaned sons": from cradle to grave, the former Soviet Union literally teems with them. Having no living God to turn to, the Russian Orthodox Church (which has always served as an instrument of the state and maintains a tenuous grasp on the the-ological "establishment" even now) is not a viable alternative for most. Hence, the lingering perception that remains in this dark corner of the world: though the workers may be few, the harvest seems almost nonexistent. And yet, by His very nature, God's thoughts are not man's thoughts; and man's ways are not God's ways. The medical missionary can only plant seeds and trust in the Lord to make a way in His own time.[43]

For all the pessimism these reflections suggest, by the end of our brief stay in Siberia a few seedlings seemed to have grown beside this rocky path lined with thistles. To nurture their growth is what brings God's workers back: seedlings such as a closed Bible (courtesy of the Gideons) that mysteriously appeared on top of the Chief of Neurosurgery's radiology view box on the third day of my visit—pointedly left open to the Beatitudes in Matthew by the sixth day; or the appearance of a small crucifix around Sasha's neck by the end of the first week that supplanted the stone amulet he was wearing when I arrived.

Rice-bowl Christians? Perhaps. I have no way of knowing whether these fledgling sprouts I had noticed have grown—or sim-ply wilted—in the chilling environs of this remote outpost of mother Russia. Maybe that's all the missionary can legitimately expect for his or her efforts. Whether its people will ever experience the blessing of being called "sons of God" is His call to make.

Great Is Your Reward in Heaven

"Blessed are those who are persecuted because of righteousness." Or for whatever reason; righteous or not, our souls cry out for an explanation as to why we are made to suffer. That's human nature. Any persecution both here and abroad that I had experienced, of course, was no match for what the Kosovar refugees suffered at the hands of the Serbs. Theirs was persecution of the most despicable sort—and somewhat far removed from what Jesus was referring to in the Beatitudes. After all, the eighth and ninth of these blessings were intended to comfort those who were reviled and persecuted for *His* sake. Needless to say, that would hardly appeal (or apply) to the Muslim mindset.

As for my own state of mind at the time, the futility of our mission there seemed to have one vicarious "redeeming" feature: if the Kosovars had been cast adrift in a tidal wave of indifference to their plight, then surely I (who had been pretentious enough to believe we could make a difference in the name of a Christian God they understandably loathed) deserved to be dragged on board their sinking ship with them. That's because I had my own demons to wrestle with back home. I had not yet reconciled myself to those who were persecuting me in my practice when I left for Albania. Nor could I forgive others responsible for a far greater suffering my father was experiencing. All of which underscores the previously expressed point that one cannot be at war with self, then drag God into it, and still expect to be an effective peacemaker on His behalf.

This brings me in a rather circuitous fashion to the Lord's inexplicable grace and the affirmation I paradoxically received at His expense, despite having disobeyed Jesus' clear command to make the best of a bad situation. Just after deciding at the last moment to go to Albania (and, it should be said, with no time spent in prayer seeking God's direction), my father had injured his back while laboring to pick my stepmother up off the floor following a fall. Both ended up in the emergency room that day—she with a badly bruised jaw, and Dad with a debilitating herniated disc. That was the sad culmination of a trying two years for my father, who had been attempting to care for his wife in the home following her diagnosis of rapidly progressive Alzheimer's disease. The time had come to put her in a nursing home, and I subconsciously knew Dad would not surrender if left to do that alone. Yet I had already tentatively made a commitment to go to Albania. With a heavy heart, he insisted that I go—assuring me that he could manage until my return.

Once in Albania, I continued to perseverate on what I perceived as abandonment of my father to do God's work. Having surmised there was no profitable work to be done (much less any harvest to be reaped on His behalf), my guilt accelerated exponentially. By the evening of the third day, I was as depressed as many of the refugees I had been futilely ministering to in the clinic. That night I couldn't sleep, torn between my commitment there and my obligations back home. Was it to be God—or family? As ever, I turned to the Bible for guidance.

Leafing through Matthew, I stumbled across a passage that brought fresh new insight to my predicament. "And everyone who has left houses or brothers or sisters or *father* [emphasis mine]...for my sake, will receive a hundred times as much and inherit eternal life" (Matthew 19:29). Oh, how I yearned to strengthen my love relationship with Jesus! Practical experience, of course, had already taught me that relationships are nourished through communication. To God, this means prayer. Now that He had me on my knees, I knew the Lord was speaking to me. How, then, was I to manifest that love in action? The New Testament is replete with verses on this very point: One must obey.

No doubt the timeless truth of God's Word that was staring back at me clearly implied I had no choice in the matter. Up until then I had sweated blood during the early morning hours—just as Christ had literally done the night before facing His greatest test. At length I found the answer for which I was searching, as had Jesus: not my will, but God's will be done. At 4:00 A.M. I turned in, fully committed to staying on.

The timing of this particular decision, however, betrays a recurring glitch in my Christian walk—one that continues to frustrate my best intentions even to this day. You see, my quiet time with the Lord is invariably late at night, largely because my physiology dictates that. I'm simply not a morning person. Consequently, God's instructions always seems so much more enlightening at night before I go to bed.

The morning is all too often another matter. Things are paradoxically darker for me then, and His direction not quite so clear. That's a sad admission. If ever there were a time when a fallen man like myself would benefit from the Lord's guidance, it is when I first face the light of day, less certain of my own way and more prone to accept that I can't make it by myself. Now, in the overcast morning gloom of a farmhouse in Albania, on the other side of the world from a man who had always been there for me when I needed him, my resolve of the night before vanished. I reversed the decision I had made just two fitfully slept hours before, and hitched a ride to the coast to catch a ferry for Italy and, ultimately, home.

My precipitate action had turned one of the underlying themes of the Bible on its head: "Remember in the darkness what you once learned in the light." Like Christ at Gethsemane, I had sought God's direction in the dark and received it. Yet, like Peter, I ultimately denied my Lord three times in the light of day by ignoring His Word and clear command, abandoning His search for those lost sheep among the Kosovars, and placing the needs of my earthly father above my Father in Heaven. I was as low as I ever remember being in my Christian walk. Having reverted to a crawl, my hasty retreat threatened to become a rout; for I was now very much alone, with nothing but a knapsack on my back, guitar in hand, and no ticket to make my way to Rome and catch a flight to New York on standby. "Ample retribution," I remember thinking "for one who has denied His Lord and gone his own way!"

So I flagellated myself during that lonely voyage home, the first leg of which began with foolishly booking passage on a rug merchant's sloop across the Adriatic. That proved to be frightening as well, once I discovered at mid-crossing that the Albanian captain, with whom I could only communicate through hand signals (and American dollars) was an arms merchant in disguise! Tucked within his rugs ostensibly for sale were AK47s and rocket launchers. Had he perceived me to be some sort of Serbian agent, my Christian walk might just as easily have ended with baptism by immersion of a different sort—one thousand feet under and lashed to a stone, dying to self in the most literal sense of the word in the middle of the Adriatic.

I'm thankful to relate that the Lord provided for my safety. I survived the crossing, but not before—as a disobedient, modern-day Jonah fleeing Nineva where God had directed him to go—being swallowed up by a "whale" of my own making. Spiritually I was in the darkness of its belly; yet just as happened to Jonah, some three days later I was "resurrected" to resume the Lord's work. That was but the first of many unmerited blessings He would bestow once I arrived home, physically exhausted and an emotional wreck. Through His grace alone, Jesus guided my steps in securing a nursing home placement for my stepmother, assuaging my father's guilt in so doing, and last (but by no means least) ministering to him physically. By now Dad's pain had become intractable and his partial paralysis progressive. He agreed to undergo surgery, and asked me to perform it. With the Lord's guidance, the surgery went well and his pain and leg weakness disappeared.

I had misread Jesus' intentions from the very beginning. No mystery there; you may recall that I had spent virtually no time in prayer seeking His will before going to Albania. This was His way of telling me now: "Just because you perceive a need, don't automatically assume that you're the one to meet it. Be *called* before you act; otherwise you may miss a more important mission I have for you to fulfill." What He clearly had in mind was ministering to my Dad first. In characteristic fashion, Christ gave me the opportunity to serve my father at the expense of the work I *thought* I had been called to do elsewhere for His own.

Yet that was hardly the end of the grace the Lord extended to me at a time when I least deserved it. Having fulfilled the criteria of His first Beatitude, "poor in spirit," through no fault but my own, Jesus inexplicably blessed me beyond measure—far and above being able to be a servant to Dad physically. Now He had another treasure in store for both of us, despite my father facing a second crisis so cruel in its implications that even now I have difficulty grasping it.

When he remarried some twenty years ago after the respective deaths of my mother and Mimi's husband, Dad had agreed to sell our home and possessions and move into her house. That proved to be a satisfactory arrangement (not to mention an endearing relationship) for eighteen years. *Four* days after moving Mimi into the nursing home, however, and just two days after his operation, her sons demanded that he move out and find another place to live! Still in the acute convalescent stage of his surgery, and with nowhere to go, Dad agreed to move in with me until a more permanent arrangement could be made.

By both of our admissions, that proved to be the richest blessing the Lord could bestow on two sheep of His pasture. Our heretofore loving (though often too distant) relationship flourished in the sharing of a home together again. We were like kids left unattended in a candy store, all the while trying to reconcile our good fortune! Why had we been given the chance so late in life to renew those intimate ties that all too often fray and unravel over time? How can one describe the joy of having a father greet his son each morning with hot coffee and a bagel to be shared over conversation before heading off to work? What can possibly match returning home in the early evening to sit down together and recount the day's events, share a laugh or two, and then tuck Dad into bed, with soft strains of Jimmy Dorsey or Benny Goodman wafting up from the radio in his bedroom below to the landing where I studied?

That's affirmation—and through no other instrument than God's grace. Servant and dispossessed had met each other on the road somewhere down in the valley, only to climb to the mountaintop and sing His praises! Blessed indeed were we that halcyon summer; for great was our reward in God's Kingdom here on earth—and will remain so beyond the Great Divide.

◦━━◦

Two years later Dad was diagnosed with terminal cancer that had spread to his spine. By his own admission, that's a painful way to die. Yet through the lens of a steadfast faith that diffused his suffering like a prism, he endured it as a small price to pay. After all, Popo knew the trials and tribulations of this life were drawing to a close, and eternity in the presence of his Father beckoned. And that, most assuredly for my own father, was not simply a wish to be convinced; rather, it is the Son of God's *promise*. What's more, Jesus had already made good on that through His own incomparable suffering, only to be resurrected to life everlasting, as Dad knew he too would be.

This is hardly to discount the formidable armamentarium of painkillers that my father received to assuage his suffering, the benefit of which Jesus did not have to lighten His own burden. Yet this much Dad and I knew we would face sooner, rather than later: my ministrations as his physician would fail him in the end. Death, orchestrated by God's mercy at a time of His choosing, would win. And Christ, as his divine and omnipotent Physician, would be there to comfort him, just as He has done for all Believers through the ages at the moment of their passing.

As befits my nature, of course—once the two of us are reunited—I fully intend to confirm that none of my father's hopes were unfounded, particularly toward the end when a combination of sleep deprivation and drugs clouded his vision. Regrettably, he had spent the very night of his passing in a quiet delirium for the

100

most part, scribbling nonexistent figures in his checkbook one moment, warily eyeing the "spiders crawling all over the ceiling" the next. At length, he settled back into a light sleep. After a minute or two, I approached his bed, leaned over, and tapped him on the chest. "Popo, there's something I need to tell you," I whispered, my voice quavering with emotion. With that, his eyes flew open—and for the first time in hours, they shone with a resolute clarity that defied his moribund condition.

"Dad, I want you to know what you've meant to all of the grateful patients you treated during your forty years as their doctor; but more important, what you've meant to my brother and me. If our lives are to reflect Jesus as a role model, then take my word for it: you've been the very best likeness of Him that I've ever known."

With his eyes fixed squarely on mine, and in a clear, resonant voice, he replied: "Bert, that's the finest compliment a father can receive from his son."

And the greatest gift that God's Son could have given me. He drew back the curtain of impending death just long enough to bring closure to our relationship by allowing me to say what every man yearns to tell his father—and to *know* it had been received! At that moment I realized, as both physician and son, I hadn't failed him after all. Nor had Christ—of that much I was certain. For great is Dad's reward in heaven—as mine, too, shall be. By His grace alone.

Closing Arguments

The Upper Room

Cultivating a taste for missions work abroad can be a tough row to hoe unless the fruit it bears comes from the vine of a truly sanctified life. Perhaps that's why God brought Don McCormick into the field where I labored five years ago to restake and fertilize the shallow taproot of my faith, having just been reborn and grafted into the body of Christ. Don was well into reaping his own harvest for the Lord back home when I first met him at Camino, a men's spiritual retreat. Putting his shoulder to my plow, we navigated the freshly tilled (if manifestly uneven) rows of my Christian walk together—he with that deft touch of the Master's hand, breaking through the bedrock of my resistant past.

Our shared endeavor was no coincidence; God has a way of arranging such relationships. These divine appointments are vitally important to Him. After all, it's not so much the work we bear as the relationship we share with one another—and with Jesus—that matters. As but one measure of His grace, I was able to minister in kind to Don a year later—if only in a physical sense. He had been diagnosed with brain cancer, and I was entrusted with removing it. Hardly to Jesus' surprise, Don bore his own cross joyfully every step

of the way. As for myself, a modern-day Simon of Cyrene in surgeon's dress, I merely shouldered his burden temporarily on those
rare occasions when he tired.

Jesus had been Don's vine from the beginning. Now He was
being called into service as the Great Physician and, needless to say,
performed admirably. Any contribution I made toward nursing my
friend back to health was minuscule compared to the power of His
healing hand. Having applied the bandages for Jesus in the operating room, I simply stepped aside as He made good on his promise
to heal Don physically. That was but a foretaste of the lush banquet
the Lord was preparing for myself and countless others during His
disciple's convalescence in the Upper Room.

It was there that Jesus laid out the meal and organized the celebration. Don obediently "bused tables" by dispensing the Bread of
Life to hungry souls who visited him at his bedside. No account
more humbly underscores that than a subsequent testimonial he
made on his Father's behalf a year and a half later. Yet even now,
I'm not certain how truly aware Don was of its take-home message
for the care-giver: ministering to others in the mission field is a
two-way street. Whether at home or abroad, the patient is Jesus'
most powerful witness. They shall know Him by its fruit.

⚫━✦━⚫

In truth, Don would probably be the first to acknowledge that
he was not the principal author of the script. As God's tested servant, his perspective bore the unmistakable imprint of the Holy
Spirit—what one might even term "divine inspiration." Before dis-
missing that as mere hyperbole, the skeptic would do well to weigh
the evidence. For one thing, the text reads like a Pauline letter in
modern-day vernacular, emphasizing as it does Don's triumph
through Christ's personal presence in His life. Even that might
seem outlandish on the face of it; physicians who treat such malig-
nancies as brain cancers know they are bound to recur. To proclaim
victory while still playing that daunting hand would compel the
realists among us to suspect a stacked deck.

Which is precisely the point. You see, Don knows the dealer
intimately. His name is Jesus. What distinguishes Him from other

dealers is that the Lord allows those who play by the Father's rules an occasional peek into His hand. Intent as Don was at the time in nurturing his love-relationship with Jesus through an exhaustive study of the resurrection, he had become as one with his Lord. A "time of spiritual unity" is how he described it. Like King David, Don had become a man seeking after God's own heart.

Little did my friend anticipate, however, that he would be granted the privilege of distinctively hearing God speak. Make no mistake; Don was very much aware of Who was doing the talking, because the sheep of the Lord's pasture know His voice. Reflecting on that later, my friend succinctly reconciled his good fortune: "When you truly seek to know God, He seeks you out in turn by taking you to a higher level of understanding." Not that Don liked what he had been told. For one so musically challenged, God's commandment that he sing to his Sunday school class seemed patently absurd. "So what's your point, son?" one can imagine his Father replying. "I don't make it a practice to choose the gifted; I gift the chosen. Take it or leave it, but the one thing you mustn't do is argue. Just trust me."

Only a stuttering sheepherder by the name of Moses had successfully argued with God by putting his own life on the line for the disobedient children of Israel in the Sinai desert. Was this soft-spoken veterinarian now willing to do the same because of a simple case of stage fright? Hardly; for Don is nothing if not a practical man. Had he felt it expedient to invoke such a scriptural precedent, he might have persisted. Yet one thing my mentor most assuredly is not: a devotee of the Old Testament. To his way of thinking, it was no longer necessary (much less prudent) to argue with God, because He had already given His final Word. Twice, in fact: once to all mankind in the form of His Son ("In the beginning was the Word...");[44] now to Don alone ("It won't change anything if I have to tell you again").

The first Word was all His good and faithful servant had ever needed to hear anyway. In a flash, Don put aside what work he was doing for God, and went downstairs instead to where God was working. As ever, Jesus had preceded him and prepared the way. There, staring mutely at him from his computer screen, was the

Scripture he had already been given to memorize that week: "If you love me, keep my commandments." Enough said. This chastened disciple did just as he was told.

Why such a precipitate surrender? No mystery there; Don was intimately familiar with the greatest commandment of all: love God with all your heart, mind, and soul, which He equates with obedience. Was it any coincidence that His Son, immediately before interceding on my friend's behalf during the days ahead, would focus on the heart by first testing Don's response to God's greatest commandment? Not at all. A disciple's heart must bear the stamp of the Holy Spirit if it is to bear in kind what Christians recognize as "sanctified" fruit: sanctified, because God reaps His most bountiful harvests through tested disciples who share His vision; sanctified, because that reflects the experience of His only begotten Son, who had obeyed His Father to the letter; sanctified, because Don himself would have to wear a crown of thorns before ever presuming to wear the crown of glory.

No doubt God had chosen the right man for the job. For one thing, my mentor was well past being simply a born-again Christian. The phrase "born again to a new life in Christ" means exactly what it says; it's only a beginning. As Don's lengthy Christian walk so richly exemplified, however, life thereafter is spent emptying one's self completely and filling the void with the Holy Spirit that Jesus bequeathed to all Believers at the ascension. And being remade in His image takes time. To be made to suffer in the process, of course, "raises the bar"; after all, dying to self is painful. Yet that's precisely what Christ had done, what the apostle Paul rejoiced in—and what my friend now subconsciously anticipated.

He didn't have long to wait. Two weeks later Don heard the Lord's voice a second time, commanding him to make amends with a man who had grievously wronged his family. God was taking him to the next level of obedience embodied in the second greatest commandment: "Love your neighbor as yourself." Now, it's one thing to worship a loving God in the light—quite another to forgive an enemy in the darkness of a wounded soul. With a sullen heart, God's faithful servant nevertheless again did exactly as he was told. The response from his antagonist was as overwhelming as it was unexpected: "Don, I forgive you." You could have heard an angel's voice, echoing in the recesses of a grateful heart . . . . "It was if the Lord had expressed his total forgiveness to me through the mouth of my enemy," he recalled.

Shortly thereafter, Don's final and most difficult test began— one that threatened his physical well-being far more than it could ever deter his spiritual walk. He pondered the reason why, after so many intensive studies of God's Word, His Father had chosen this particular time to speak to him. Don had always been a little skeptical of others' claims to such divine encounters anyway, though that was certainly no deterrent when his time came. Yet the "why" was another matter. "The only thing I could think of was that God was getting ready to take me home," he confided, "and had some things He wanted me to do to get ready." Perhaps my mentor's penchant for ignoring the Old Testament served him poorly in this one instance, which a paraphrase from the book of Proverbs (3:2-5) makes all too clear: Don't depend on your own mind for understanding; rather, trust God to reveal what He has in mind for you.

Not only would Don be proven wrong on his first assumption that he was about to die; the second merely affirmed the preparation he had been making all along. No, the Lord had little need to steel His disciple for something as trivial as a brain operation, much less, death; those messy details Jesus had already promised to handle on His own. Rather, He was intent upon preparing Don for a triumphant return to the mission field with the most compelling Christian witness imaginable.

Once more the Lord preceded him there and prepared the way. He had begun by refocusing Don's attention on God's two greatest commandments. Thereafter, Jesus brought His Christian community to bear as a supporting cast for our friend's upcoming ministry. Not that we were particularly gifted as Curers; that would have been superfluous. Yet as Carers we had been given one gift of inestimable value: hands that held on to the same anointed one Don would grasp during his walk through the valley in the shadow of death. For Jesus knows that the only arms God has to embrace His children—and the only hands He has with which to lead us— are our own.

Now, arms and hands are but one "extension" of the divine anatomy of which we have been so wondrously and gloriously made. Others lead inwardly to the heart—such as eyes to see His presence and ears to hear the Good News. To Don's credit, he had nurtured both senses so assiduously through the years that his pastor's explanation for what he was now up against—physical disability as an anticipated part of life and not to be feared, discipline which is used to teach and not to punish, and trials that must be faced in order to glorify God—came as yet another immediate, affirming revelation.

Such insights, of course, usually fall on deaf ears among unbelievers and nominal Christians. I know that from experience. I've been there, done that—and failed despite my best intentions. Only as one reborn in Christ do I now understand why. As the old saying goes, "it's all in the eye of the beholder." How often had similar "assurances" come across as patronizing, even condescending, to those patients and families who had long since closed their eyes (and ears) to the timeless truth of His Word and His promises—or had never opened them to begin with.

Don reacted altogether differently: "Suddenly I realized this was not about me at all," he exclaimed. "It was about Jesus." That hardly came as a surprise for one whose life's view consistently reflected the time-honored creed missionaries invoke to mitigate their often disappointing (and always difficult) calling: It's not for them; it's for Him! Don's subsequent prayers echoed the same theme during those dark hours before his pending surgery. "I called three Camino friends," he confided, "and solicited their prayers; not for me, but to glorify God."

Which brings me to why the book of Job had so little to teach this far from mortally wounded Christian warrior. The contrasts between my friend's predicament and that consummate sufferer of the Old Testament speak for themselves. "I chose three brothers that I knew would do what I asked," Don went on to say, "and they did." Whereas he hand-picked his friends to do a task for God, Job's friends had come with their own agendas. As disciples of Jesus, Don's intercessors focused on God; Job's, as self-appointed counselors, advised him to focus on self. Not much has changed.

Witness the same disparity in the two alternatives of counseling available today for "good" people when "bad" things happen to them: spiritually based soul-affirmation versus behaviorally based self-absorption. The problematic results of the latter approach speak to the limitations of psychological counseling in the face of catastrophic illness.

At this point in my study of Don's presentation, I began to sense a bit of déjà vu in what Christ had endured—notwithstanding those critics (and perhaps Don himself) who would hasten to point out that Jesus' three closest disciples had hardly distinguished themselves in the Garden of Gethsemane the night before He faced death. Unlike my friend's attentive companions, Peter, James, and John had fallen asleep—leaving Jesus to ponder the meaning of His upcoming trial alone. As but one measure of Don's peace of mind (for which Christ, ironically, had paid the ultimate price), the only person who rested well during the gathering storm that particular night was this Spirit-filled fisher-of-men himself. Whipped by wind yet still afloat, Don slept like a baby, secure in the knowledge that Christ Himself was in his boat....

How, then, to explain my friend's ability to navigate the shoals of impending disability, and possibly death, with such Christ-like aplomb, when Jesus had behaved under similar duress—well—so *humanly*? Simply stated, God had prepared for this very moment two thousand years ago by temporarily surrendering His exalted position in heaven to become a man like Don—to experience firsthand the suffering of the very child He had created and loves so dearly. Having completely emptied Himself of His divine attributes so as to not use them for His own advantage,[45] Jesus elected to suffer like ourselves in such a "fallen" state. Not surprisingly, He had responded as any mortal man would.

Christ's ascension some forty days later as Lord, of course, changed all that. Returning to heaven, Jesus left behind the Holy Spirit to serve as our Counselor and Comforter. Christians refer to this as being "infilled with the Holy Spirit"—the very same Spirit that Don now possessed through no merit of his own. Yet another unfathomable gift from the Father Himself is GRACE: God's Riches At Christ's Expense. This endearing phrase is our child-like way of remembering (and appropriately so, as children of God) that we have all had our ways prepared by Jesus' suffering on the cross, subsequent resurrection, and ultimate ascension. Having been crucified *with* Christ and born to new life through the infilling of His Holy Spirit, we remain today undeserving beneficiaries of God's boundless grace. That was yet another pearl I had gleaned from the pages of this modern-day Pauline epistle.

Events surrounding Don's preparation for what lay ahead evoke yet a second image, drawn from what he would term a "sacramental moment" in his life—and in the life of Christ's church by extension. I'm referring to the day of Pentecost, when the power of the Holy Spirit swept through a room of fervently praying disciples, ultimately driving them out into the streets to proclaim the Good News. It's in this sense that Don's presentation possessed the spiritual force of both the resurrection and Pentecost combined. To some that might seem an audacious claim. Before passing judgment, let me explain.

The night before his surgery, several of Don's friends escorted him to the hospital chapel for some quiet prayer and fellowship. By his own admission, Don neither knew what to pray for nor even remembers what prayers were offered. What he does recall, however, was the distinct presence of the Holy Spirit. That was, after all, what he had a right to expect; for God had promised to both direct and then answer the prayers of a righteous man, just as Christ's prayer on the cross was ultimately answered by His resurrection and ascension to the Father's right hand. "I just asked the Holy Spirit to intervene for me and give to God the prayers of my heart," Don recalled, "so that He might be glorified." Once again the Lord made good on His promise to a very righteous man. The end result? Both got what they desired—and deserved: God *was* exalted, and the Holy Spirit touched everyone present in the chapel that night.

The Spirit's presence spilled over into the following morning as friends, family, and church members from all over southwest Missouri inundated Don's room. They created such a commotion that the entire flock was asked to move down to the waiting room. Answering the Lord's call, they just kept coming, filling yet a second room on another floor. Emotions reached such a pitch that an impromptu praise and worship service resulted, reuniting all of us together again in one place. There we linked hands in a huge, swaying circle—joined to the same Hand that was now leading Don through a valley no longer dark, but positively glowing, in the reflection of the Christ- light.

That was the most visible manifestation of what Don would later use as a title for his talk: "Christian Community in Action." Yet those who were there sensed they had experienced something more—Pentecost revisited—in (of all places) the sterile environs of a modern hospital. The only thing that distinguished this event from what happened in Jerusalem was the absence of skeptics suggesting that perhaps we had all consumed too much wine! At least I could vouch for my own sobriety, ruefully acknowledging the sobering work still to be done downstairs.

Still a third image emerges from the pages of my friend's script—which, in characteristic fashion, Don would humbly reject altogether. I'm speaking of the Last Supper in the Upper Room, during which the cup and bread were shared between Christ and His disciples, including the "one whom Jesus loved." Now, it so happens that Don has such a special friend, one who also happens to possess the spiritual gift of prophecy. The two soul mates drank from the cup and broke bread that night, alone in the darkness with their Cokes, chocolate bars, and thoughts. Whereas scholars continue to debate whether Christ's disciples understood the symbolism of the cup and bread that fateful evening in Jerusalem, Don clearly appreciated what his friend foresaw: God was in control, preparing him to enter new and uncharted territory in the mission field.

Whether he would bear a "thorn in the flesh" thereafter as a token of that commitment was up to the Father. Either way, Don harbored no fears of abandonment by his Christian friends, nor any doubt that he would see them again. Yet Jesus had laid one burden on his heart: strapped to a gurney on his way to surgery the following morning, my friend could not help but reflect on those lost sheep he might not have reached in time—just as Christ Himself no doubt had been aware as He shouldered the cross on His way to Golgotha, surrounded by a throng of unbelievers.

Nor would it be over-dramatizing the point to compare the environment in which Don found himself at the moment he underwent his general anesthetic to what the Christian is promised when crossing over the Great Divide: no fear, no pain, no abandonment, not even silence. Christ had borne all of that on his behalf already. Surrounded by a supportive operating team of brothers and sisters, soothed by the strains of praise and worship music echoing from somewhere above, God's favored son drifted off to sleep, eagerly anticipating his rebirth.

Eight hours later, the stone was rolled away. As Don emerged from the tomb of his waning anesthesia in the company of a host of angels disguised as recovery-room nurses, Jesus was there to tenderly embrace him. But not before the Lord had personally ministered to the remainder of His flock in the waiting room during the necessary separation required to usher their brother back through the narrow gate. As ever, God had kept His promise. My only contribution to the whole affair came later that evening through a song I imposed on Don and Vicki, whose lyrics gave much greater solace to them, I'm sure, than did my fumbling fingers on the guitar:

> "Christ asleep within my boat,
> Whipped by winds yet still afloat.
> Joy is like the rain."

That amateurish performance understandably paled in comparison to the impact on those nurses who stared in wonderment as their charge, having just undergone a brain operation, responded by singing "God is so good; He's so good to me" in a clear, resonant voice. So as to reciprocate, Jesus arose from some much needed slumber at the back of the boat, goading me to play one of the few other songs I knew at the time. God may work in mysterious ways, but this much was crystal clear: surely the presence of the Lord was in this place....

One final impression remains to embellish the cornerstone that my friend laid for his Lord and Savior that week. A Christian is known by the fruit he bears—and during his remaining two days in the hospital, Don had a harvest-full perched atop that stone for all to see. Not the least of which were the testimonies of every health-care worker with whom he came in contact. Witnessing a resurrection of sorts was one thing; experiencing the power of Pentecost quite another! Various paramedical personnel manufactured excuses to come into Don's room to sense the presence of something that most could not put into words. It was left to one of the sheep of Christ's flock to speak for them: "The sweet smell of the Holy Spirit is in this room."

And so He was. Which explains my friend's unimaginable reaction to it all: "That was the best week of my life!" Remarkable words indeed—not so much on account of Don having emerged "whole" from what he had just been through, but because of his refusal to take credit for the fruit it bore on behalf of everyone else. To Don's way of thinking, nothing but the grace of God and a vigilant Christian community in action had been responsible. As such, the most fervent prayer of a very righteous man had been answered after all.

⊙═╾╀╼═⊙

With such a comforting benediction, perhaps that should have been the end of the matter. Yet for many readers who still find themselves on the bubble spiritually, a hint of gloss lingers over what some might dismiss as a Norman Rockwell caricature. I understand that; there was a time when I could not possibly have perceived reality as I do today. That's the first in a long list of belated confessions I need to make. The best education imaginable, and the rewards of a lucrative neurosurgical practice, had sublimated any need to examine the Bible dispassionately to prove (or disprove) the reality of Jesus. After all, things were just fine in my life. Why stir up the waters with something as esoteric as God? No telling what undercurrents that might create to rock my boat—or swamp it altogether!

From the Christian perspective, that is precisely the point. It's called "dying to self"; to be reborn with Christ through baptism in the very image of God that each of us was originally conceived.

"Total surrender," "walking in faith," "having eyes to see and ears to hear;" all are variations on the theme that Don's life so richly personified. By way of contrast, what little there was to show for my own included a dog-eared study Bible heavily annotated with "marginalia," a wealth of noble intentions—and a few nagging questions. I was still trying to tie up all those loose ends! That was yet another burden I laid on my friend's shoulders long after our shared experience in the hospital—as if he hadn't enough to bear already.

In spite of every spiritual truth that Don's Christian walk had already revealed to me, I never quite surrendered the vainglorious notion that I had something to offer him in return: that all my study had some redeeming value; that I might have stumbled upon a new perspective which would somehow benefit my mentor. A mere two hours of conversation one evening at his home, however, divested me of my pretensions. I simply had to confess that all my books and acquired beliefs were no match for Don's experience and enduring faith.

Perhaps I should have first considered that age-old adage, "The road to failure is paved with good intentions." To compound the offense, mine was pot-holed with bad imitations. I proved a far better likeness of the brash side of Peter (seldom right, but never in doubt!) than I was of my Lord and Savior. Just as Jesus knew his disciples' hearts and minds better than they knew their own, Don had already anticipated every angle I pursued. His responses were as succinct and to the point as my questions were open- ended and filled with commentary.

To be sure, he occasionally accommodated my half-baked ideas merely to be polite (as always befitted his nature)—but never when they conflicted with what he *knew* to be true. Not that there was ever a hint of a "Get behind me, Satan" rebuke in what Don said; only quiet and steadfast confidence that comes with having surrendered his own pretensions to the Lord long ago. For you see, my humble friend had simply chosen to stand on Jesus' promises, and reaped the benefits accordingly.

As Don so aptly put it: "Total surrender on our part engenders total grace on God's" (not to mention wisdom, as quickly became apparent). He was referring, of course, to the triune God of the

New Testament. Only Jesus provides Don total affirmation and total security. Only the Holy Spirit speaks through him and to others on the Lord's behalf. And only God is Father to both. On those points Don never wavered despite my best efforts to convince him of the value of the Old Testament.

What I perceived as a frightfully narrow perspective was difficult for me to understand at first—until I tumbled to the realization during our exchange of views that I was faced with a disciple totally at peace with himself and his faith. That became apparent once I asked Don about any setbacks he may have encountered during his own Christian walk (and to which all of us are subject, if the Psalms are any indication). Or so I prefaced the question. My reference to the Old Testament as an aside proved an inauspicious opening move: not only had Don never experienced any setbacks that he could recall; if the Psalms had relevance for his faith at all, it was to supply an apt phrase or two in moments of prayer.

Make no mistake; my friend is eternally grateful for the word-pictures the Psalmist provided. He reminded me, however, that David neither knew Jesus when he wrote them, nor did he have benefit of the Holy Spirit bequeathed to Believers following Christ's ascension. To his way of thinking, that explains why the majority of the Psalms reflects the writer's doubts and disappointments—not the joy Don was experiencing day to day.

Making no progress there, I inquired as to my mentor's best definition of the word "faith" (taking the opportunity, in characteristic fashion, to have slipped in one that I particularly liked; i.e., "Being sure of what you hope for, and certain of what you cannot see"). His definition was far more succinct, framed in a single word: "Jesus."

"But," I countered, "doesn't the Old Testament at least provide the necessary historical background that presages, and then sustains, our belief that Jesus was and is the Messiah?" Though the question betrayed my own need for validation, Don is well past that. He's been in the affirmation mode for so long that this was the stuff of ancient history for him. Anything antedating the coming of Jesus was simply irrelevant to his present Christian walk. For Don, the Kingdom—and all the blessings that it confers—is now.

Refusing to surrender the point entirely, I cited Moses' greatest disappointment at the end of his life as an apt historical parallel to what might lay ahead for my friend and patient: specifically, whether he might have any regrets about his brain cancer cutting him off too soon before "seeing" the Promised Land during his physical life here on earth.

Don saw no merit in the comparison. He had never viewed the Promised Land from some sort of mountaintop, as Moses had done before he died; rather, he was experiencing it first-hand down in the valley where (as he reminded me) "the lilies grow, neither toiling nor spinning"—for none was clothed as richly as he is today in the warmth of Jesus' embrace and his extended Christian family of Believers.

Point taken. Still, there were other parallels I thought Don needed to consider. For one, Moses had been the only man in recorded history who had won an argument with God, ultimately convincing Him to change His mind regarding the fate of those obstinate Israelites in the Sinai desert. I wondered whether that compared favorably (or unfavorably, depending on point of view) to the night Don had argued with God about being made to sing to his Sunday school class.

As usual, my mentor was way ahead of me. "Perhaps a comparison with Jacob, who had been the only man to have *wrestled* with God, would be more fitting," he responded chuckling, "particularly when you consider the end result." Shifting gears, we quickly reviewed the story in Genesis together. Upon reflection, I had to admit the parallels were striking.

To begin with, God had never tired during the hours-long match with this Old Testament patriarch, ample testimony to the fact that He could have defeated his adversary at any time He chose to, and taken Jacob's life if that had been His will. Instead, God allowed him to continue wrestling simply for the sake of receiving His blessing: that his brother, Esau, might forgive Jacob for having cheated him out of his birthright years earlier. At length, the Lord ended the match by dislocating Jacob's hip in exchange for the sought-after blessing. Limping off, the wounded patriarch evinced nothing but grateful thanks for God's mercy. Shortly thereafter,

Jacob built an altar to commemorate the new name (Israel) he had been given as a reminder of his own weakness, God's power, and a blessing that only He could give.

Nodding in response, I now understood where Don was leading me. He too had continued to "wrestle" with God during those fateful early morning hours before surrendering in obedience. What's more, the Lord never answered him as such ("It won't change anything if I have to tell you again"), just as God had responded to Jacob's inquiry as to His identity with only a rhetorical question. And as a modern-day Jacob, Don would bear the cancer that was discovered shortly thereafter as little more of a burden than had he sustained a dislocated hip! For my friend knew full well that he at least had received His Lord's blessing.

Everything that my mentor said seemed to fit hand in glove— except the last statement. I had trouble envisioning a malignant brain tumor as a "blessing," much less that God would "give" such an illness to any person, regardless of the reason. Don agreed; yet the times were different before Jesus came, he reminded me, and that makes all the difference in the world:

> God does not do anything bad to his children today. Yet in the Old Testament He did, because the people were under a different covenant—a *conditional* one to be exact. There was a price to pay for sin. But we don't have to be punished now for the same offense. Jesus took care of that for us. We're under a new covenant that took the place of the old. And that, you see, is the blessing.

Which left me with only one question to ask: "Like Jacob, have you built an altar to the Lord in thanksgiving?"

Pointing to his heart, Don replied: "I didn't build it, but this is my altar."

Unaware at the time just how prophetic that would prove to be a year or so after our conversation that evening,[46] I turned to one of my favorite Christian apologists, Philip Yancey, for support. Now that Don had at least acknowledged the Old Testament with his reference to Jacob, I wondered whether my friend had read *The*

Bible That Jesus Read. This certainly enhanced my own understanding of Jesus' exposure to Scripture (i.e., the Old Testament) and consequent perspectives that characterized His later ministry.

Alas; to no avail. While agreeing that the whole purpose of Old Testament Scripture was to set the stage for God's ultimate solution for sin after the Fall, Don felt he already knew all the history he needed to know: the Father had sent His only begotten Son on our behalf. What's more, my friend already knows Jesus—intimately— and through grace alone has all the security he requires to nurture that relationship. Having acknowledged Jesus as the object of Old Testament prophecy long ago, there was little value in having some other source "document" that for him now.

"Yet what about those who are still searching"? I asked. Or simply waiting, for that matter—refreshing his memory with some familiar refrains from the Good Book that seemed to pose all the right questions, including a few we continue to ask today such as "Does God Care?"

Graciously ignoring my acute memory lapse in view of what he had just told me (shades of Peter revisited!), Don exclaimed without hesitation: "You bet He does! Why else would He have surrendered a part of Himself for recalcitrants like ourselves? Only the Father can know the pain of such a loss—the ultimate price He paid." He then went on to add that we shouldn't expect to find answers for our own suffering anywhere in the Old Testament, much less in the book of Job.

That struck a responsive chord—and, I don't mind admitting, a painful one. I was taken aback. Given my pedagogical mindset, I thought I knew a thing or two about suffering, having written a book on the subject as seen through the experiences of several families of patients I had ministered to who had wrestled with catastrophic neurological illness in one of their own.[47] Indeed, each chapter had begun with a heading taken from Job, the acknowledged "Bible" on suffering. "How," I wondered aloud, "can one truly understand a man's suffering and his response to it, if that doesn't include liberal references to the book of Job?"

At least that's the current perception of how to address the problem, if the popularized approach of Harold Kushner[48] is any indication. "And while we're at it," I added, "how does the hack-neyed Christian response 'Jesus is the answer!' apply to the matter at hand?" Which brings to mind that equally hackneyed response of the skeptic: 'So what's the question? '" I suspect we've all asked the same thing at one time or another. Now seemed an appropri-ate time to deal with both issues as one in relation to suffering. I asked Don if he could give me the benefit of his perspective.

"Look at it this way," he began; "Kushner is Jewish. As such, his theology is strictly Old Testament." He then went on to explain the apparent contradiction between Christianity and Judaism in their respective responses when bad things happen to good people:

> The implication dividing the two is that the Old Testa-ment God is vengeful, whereas the New Testament God is compassionate. And in one respect, there is a differ-ence in perspective, but probably not what Kushner had in mind. You see, the Old Covenant appeals to a mes-siah-in-waiting; the New Covenant to a messiah who has already come. They simply didn't have a messiah in the Old Testament like we have today—in particular, one who suffered with them. Because a very bad thing happened to this very good person. And that, you see, is why Jesus is the answer.

As for the cynical question I referred to earlier, the logical choice had to be "Does God Care?" after all—because He suffered with us and for us. In that sense, the God of the Old and New Testaments are no different. Father and Son are one.

"If there is any difference at all," Don explained, "that entails to Whom we choose to respond. Whereas secular man is always look-ing for the missing link, whether in defense of evolution or the despair of agnosticism, the fact of the matter is, there is one ever-present link. His name is Jesus, the tie that binds the triune God of the Old and New Covenants. Jesus came from God and gave us Himself. It's the very best—and final—answer His Father could give. Poor Job simply was not availed of that gift; hence, he had no answer for his suffering then, and can offer none for our own today."

As convincing as Don's explanation was, I still found myself somehow *limiting* Jesus in terms of His ability to provide all the answers. For one, there are still a lot of unfulfilled prophecies floating around out there, and I challenged my mentor on that point. "Then what," I asked, "do we make of those timeless refrains of the Old Testament prophets, such as 'Why doesn't God Act?' or 'How long, Oh Lord?'—particularly when those pleas were followed by four hundred years of silence?"

No mystery for Don there: for one thing, he doesn't believe that even the most fervent prayers of unbelievers (as pertains to God *or* Jesus) are heard, except for prayers of profession and/or confession. For another, given the proclivity of mankind to ignore that elemental truth in Old Testament times, God simply waited as long as He could before acting decisively through His Son—and for the last time before the end times.

The response in the interim, he reminded me, is up to us: "Not only is that but one aspect of His Story worth remembering; it's the only aspect of history worth acting upon!" Don had obviously taken that to heart long ago, just as Christ had done for him in total surrender, obedience, and humility. Without a hint of arrogance, my friend then volunteered by way of affirmation that "the prayers of a righteous man avail much—and I *am* a righteous man. Not a perfect man, and not even good; but one who has been made righteous by Christ's finished work on the cross." This confirmed in Don's mind what his Father had been saying all along: there is no substitute for walking the walk.

As for myself, sad to relate, I was still caught up in talking the talk. Pouncing on his prior reference to the end times, I thought I had found at least one angle to successfully exploit. "But what about all this unfinished business of which the prophets spoke before Jesus returns in power and glory?"—adding for emphasis that His resurrection had not ushered in the end of history, but only the beginning of the end. After all, wasn't it my old ally Philip Yancey who had described our present predicament as something akin to a three-day Easter weekend? Just as the tragedy that befell Christ on Friday ultimately turned to triumph on Sunday, today we seem to be stuck somewhere late on Saturday, what with all those prophecies yet to be fulfilled. "At last," I thought to myself, "a reason to get Don to read Yancey's book!"

Hardly. Don has a book of his own that provides all the answers he needs, irrespective of the prophets' pleadings or my own. It's called Revelation. And it refers to Jesus' Second Coming. He succinctly argued the point: "We don't know what the future holds, but we *do* know Who holds the future." Upon further reflection, I had to agree that only the Lamb of God is capable of breaking the seal and opening the scroll of history. For Jesus had already announced the beginning of its end, in effect, when He opened another scroll in his hometown synagogue and proclaimed that Isaiah's prophecy concerning the Messiah had now been fulfilled in the listeners' presence.[49] As such, I confessed, Jesus alone is worthy of bringing history to its appropriate and final end, because it's *His* Story to complete.

So where did that leave Yancey? The answer was painfully obvious: pointing his finger right back at me. "For on that final day, the questions that plagued the Old Testament writers…, that still plague many [a Believer] today, will seem like distant memories, the kind of questions a *child* might ask" (emphasis mine). As for Don, no response was necessary; there were simply no questions left to answer! His previously expressed one-word definition of faith sufficed—and in fact had been expanded through his relationship with Jesus into a parody of my own "scholarly" definition: "Being sure of Whom you love, and certain He loves you in return." The irony at the close of our conversation was hardly lost to me: there we sat, I the obstinate child, insisting on walking in sight before I would walk in faith; and Don, the exemplary father, walking in faith so that others might see.

Perhaps it was no coincidence that during the past year of our father-son relationship I have affectionately addressed Don as "Old Man," and he addresses me as "Young Fellow"—subliminal acknowledgment that while certainly traveling the same road, we are at far different points in our respective Christian walks. Which brings to mind that poignant scene at the cross, as depicted in the Gospel of John: "When Jesus saw his mother there, and the disciple whom He loved standing nearby, He said to His mother. 'Dear woman, here is your son;' and to the disciple, 'here is your mother. '" Now, to be compared to Christ is hardly something Don would willingly accept. Yet taking some literary license to transpose the characters tells a modern-day tale that affirms the lasting legacy of one man's life as a witness. It reads like this: "When Don saw His Savior [hanging] there, and I whom he loved standing nearby, he said to Jesus. 'Dear Lord, here is your son;' and to myself as His disciple, 'Young Fellow, here is your Father....'"

Postscript

Fast forward to the last Camino spiritual retreat that Don and I attended together some four years after the first. The depth of my mentor's gratitude for what Jesus had done in his life was poignantly revealed in a reprise of the talk he had given to the participants well over a year ago. Acknowledging that (at least by medical standards) he should have passed away some time before, Don knelt in worship at the altar following his presentation and prayed: "Dear Lord, thank you for giving me the chance to tell this story one more time." To which everyone in the room responded with a chorus of heart-felt "Amens"—fully aware that our beloved friend had soundly beaten the odds through God's grace alone.

Yet the next sentence in his prayer left us gasping in wonderment: "And thank you, Lord, for giving me a story to tell." Here was a confession that no mortal man who stood apart from Jesus could possibly have uttered. The "sign" of God's blessing that Don truly believed he had been given was not a mere dislocated hip—no, not even a "thorn in the flesh." It was a malignant brain tumor! And at that very moment, God's obedient servant was on his knees, praising his Creator and Sustainer for having borne it with grace so that he might be a compelling witness for others. God may act in supernatural if often mysterious ways. That's His right. Yet how this saint responded to the challenge was, by all accounts, a supernatural "rite" of the highest order—and remains so today, four years into his ongoing battle with cancer.

Shortly thereafter, on a particularly dark day, I recall sharing with Don some of the tribulations I was facing in my practice vs. the affirmation I had been afforded in the medical mission field.

He encouraged me to focus on the Big Picture, i.e., what mattered for eternity in the eyes of God. "Remember this," he added, "Satan cannot touch your salvation; that's already been sealed through your faith in Christ. Yet the Evil One most assuredly can test your commitment, placing worldly temptations in your path to deter your Christian walk along the way. At this very moment, I believe he is using the standards of this world to steal your joy; mind you, he's the Prince of it, and everything within it is subject to his ruses."

Reflecting on Don's perspective a week or so later, I was chastened to find I had already made a very similar confession long before. As providence (or God) might have it, that surfaced among a pile of notes I had tucked away for safekeeping. Though laced with self-pity bordering on narcissism, it nevertheless reflects what I felt five years earlier when I surrendered to the Lord's call. As such, it is reproduced unedited as but one confession drawn from the life of a pilgrim whose progress to date had certainly been less than exemplary. Insofar as I was still straddling the fence professionally, what both the text and my subsequent journey *did* exemplify, I must also confess, is that the Christian walk is indeed a series of new beginnings:

> If willing to walk in faith alone, and abjuring those standards to which the secular world tells me I must conform, I can be freed from the chains that bind me to this workplace that has no eternal value: a revolving door of patients who have a wealth of neurosurgeons at their disposal to choose from. There will always be those among the latter who, for a fee, continue to fulfill their perceived roles as repairmen contracted to fix a problem, when the only binding contract is with God.
>
> Where He is sending me is altogether different. And if I'm not there to do the work, then it's not going to get done. That doesn't make me special; rather, it's simply the niche God graciously made for me to fill. He knows my heart and, far more important, those of countless sufferers elsewhere who currently have no access to what few medical skills the Lord has placed in

my hands to serve them. The "rewards" of this life (i. e. money, prestige, security) didn't matter to Jesus, and given my inborn nature, have never really had any meaning for me.

As one now newly reborn, I will listen to my Father's voice. After all, it's only the healing of souls for eternity that matters to Him. I must continue to live in this world, but that will no longer be where society and my previous life have placed me. Rather, I will dwell in <u>His</u> world, where the Holy Spirit feeds my soul—so that I might feed those whom He brings me to serve in the short time that remains.

Such, then, was the confession that ultimately brought me to the missions field, not just as an avocation, but as a calling—and with that, all the affirmation only Jesus can bring to His table beyond the Upper Room.

Death: An End or a New Beginning?

There was a time when I would have perceived my father's death and Don's struggle differently. Throughout my "first life" as a somewhat suspect Don Quixote—earnest physician, untenured historian, and self-taught medical ethicist—I was haunted by the social consequences of our failures as neurosurgeons. Eschewing the wisdom to be drawn from Ecclesiastes ("of making many books there is no end") led me to a literary failure in its own right: a book about families adversely affected by catastrophic neurological illness.[50]

Certainly their testimonials offered all the pathos necessary to capture a publishing editor's attention. As for how those fit into his obligate "human interest" formula, the downside of that equation was chock-full of unmet expectations, suffering, and despair. Yet what I could not do, in the end, was balance the scales with uplifting answers for the questions I raised on behalf of these victims. Consequently, the finished product was a marketing agent's worst nightmare: no upside; hence, no sales.

Perhaps that had less to do with my obvious shortcomings as a writer than the perspective from which I viewed these tragedies.

Only after belatedly surrendering myself and my practice to the Lord's call some three years following the book's publication did I come to understand that most of those families that survived managed to do so on the basis of what they brought to their respective experiences as Christians—not what I thought I had offered them as an empathetic humanist. Time and again, the presence of some all-knowing Counselor I never saw dispelled doubts and fears that no clinical psychologist, social worker, or even hospital chaplain could effectively address. For those who made it through had simply taken Jesus by the hand—and at His Word.

Not that they necessarily received answers to the riddle of pain and suffering from the Divine Physician; indeed, few if any ever even bothered to ask the "why." All they seemed to require was affirmation that their ordeal somehow mattered to their heavenly Father—a perspective they intuitively sensed only an incarnate God who had walked in their shoes could share. Jesus understood; He had already been there. That's why they allowed themselves to be hoisted to the shoulder of the Good Shepherd, carried clear of the cesspools pockmarking this foreboding wilderness, and returned to the familiar gated enclosure of the Lord's pasture. All that remained to mark Christ's presence during their painful journey was one pair of footprints in the desert sand. Mere sandals they were—yet stout enough to bear their burdens. That had been His promise; and this their affirmation.

Ironically, Jesus first led me to this narrow gate here at home some eight years ago when the most soul-searching enigma I have ever faced was laid at my own doorstep in the neurosurgical intensive care unit. More ironic still, that had been a nightmare revisited from twenty-five years before. During my residency training experience I had been entrusted with the care of a seventeen-year-old gymnast who had suffered a fracture-dislocation of the cervical spine that left him paralyzed from the neck down. Totally dependent on a respirator to breathe, Steve had remained frightfully aware of his irreversible disability from the beginning. Equally frightening for myself during those interminable weeks that followed, I was caught in a crossfire between a father who fought to honor his son's wish to die by having his respirator discontinued, and a mother who adamantly opposed such an irrevocable option.

As the conflict continued to fester, I found myself reflecting on the parallels between my young patient's predicament and the tragic, if enigmatic, Kurtz immortalized in Joseph Conrad's classic novella *Heart of Darkness*. Day after day, Steve's innermost thoughts remained enshrouded by impenetrable darkness, much as Kurtz had concealed his own. Peering down at a boy in bed on my daily rounds as if he were at the bottom of a dark precipice where the sun no longer shined, I sensed nothing but abject fatalism as his isolation intensified with time.

Conrad would have understood Steve's mind-set as it was now dictated by illness, just as he portrayed Kurtz's, who willingly chose his instead: "The mind of a man is capable of everything—because everything is in it, all the past as well as all the future."[51] This all too universal truth linking an innocent victim to one of fiction's most destitute characters would ultimately prove to be the greatest threat to Steve's survival; for the irrepressible end point in their respective life's views was pessimism, an awareness that they were eternally menaced—and most of all, by themselves. I prepared myself for the day when my fragile patient would fall prey irretrievably to his own heart of darkness.

Make no mistake; Conrad was certain he was not dealing with a lunatic in Kurtz's case, just as Steve's disability did not extend to his mind. Rather, both were in complete control of their faculties from beginning to end. "Believe me or not," the author wrote, "Kurtz' intelligence was perfectly clear—concentrated, it is true, upon himself with horrible intensity.... But his soul was mad. Being alone in the wilderness, it had looked within itself, and by heavens! I tell you, it had gone mad." If Steve's wilderness extended just beyond the bedrails of his stryker frame[52] in the neurosurgical step-down unit, its limited confines were oppressive enough to effect the same tragic result. For weeks his soul had struggled blindly with itself, no longer knowing either restraint nor fear; now it was bereft of faith as well. I stood by helplessly as the family disintegrated in kind over the impasse. Ultimately, Steve died—due in no small measure to my own "irreversible" disability of sorts as both a Curer and Carer. Or so I surmised.

Now, a quarter of a century later, I was being tested again, albeit for a different reason. It seems that I had learned nothing from my reflections written but three years before, at least nothing that a humanist perspective could supply. Yet in that failure was planted a seed that eventually led to my spiritual rebirth: a seed of the Holy Spirit that impregnated one very lost neurosurgeon's soul in—of all places!—the womb of another's despair.

That was the unwitting legacy I received from a twenty-five-year-old Hispanic, who had suffered an identical injury as the gymnast. For six weeks David lingered in the intensive care unit attached to a respirator to stay alive, his spinal cord severed beyond repair when his car overturned. Absent any hope of ever being able to breathe on his own, much less for meaningful return of function, David was destined to live his remaining years in total dependency on a machine. The tragedy here, as I perceived it, was that this heretofore strapping specimen of a man had survived the wreck at all. Memories of my past encounter with Steve flooded over me in waves of déjà vu: my prior reflections returned to haunt me verbatim during the ebb and flow of his successor's identical trial.

Those compelled me, in a perverse way, to compare the scene in the intensive care unit with Conrad's description of his first encounter with Kurtz in the jungle, surrounded by his macabre entourage:

> The vision seemed to enter the house with me—the stretcher, the phantom-bearers, the wild crowd of obedient worshippers, the gloom of the forest…. The beat of the drum, regular and muffled like the beating of a heart—a heart of conquering darkness. It was a moment of triumph for the wilderness, an invading and vengeful rush which, it seemed to me, I would have to keep back alone for the salvation of another's soul.[53]

Far removed from the darkness of a forbidding jungle, David's hospital bed had become his stretcher, the nurses his phantom-bearers, his family the obedient worshippers, a dimly lit corner in the step-down unit the forest gloom. Discharging rhythmically and muffled, the respirator beat on like some drum in a tribal funeral dirge.

Yet I had missed a far more significant parallel that Jesus had intended for me to draw; for my perspective was no different than what I had brought to the table a quarter of a century earlier. It would take four more years for the Holy Spirit to refocus my attention on what really mattered to David then, and what only matters today: crossing the Great Divide as a *spiritually alive* re-creation, justified and sanctified by the grace of God through Christ. And in the end, that proved to be a life-changing reality-check for a self-absorbed neurosurgeon—bequeathed by a physically spent, yet spiritually infilled, migrant worker.

In my defense, Conrad had been just as blind. It was as if we were both facing some vengeful "heart of darkness" that we felt obliged to "keep back alone for the salvation of another's soul."[54] Yet neither of us was speaking of "salvation" in the sense that our Creator had in mind. And therein lay the real reason for David's ultimate surrender, because he understood the concept far better than we did. He alone appreciated that any artificial preservation of his physical existence ran counter to his spiritual needs. Simply stated, David intuitively knew it was time to go home.

Tragically aware of his irrevocable plight and the implications of what he had been pleading with us to do throughout his ordeal, we ultimately honored David's request and discontinued the respirator. But not before dragging him down every secular blind alley in fulfilling our professional obligations to convince him otherwise. After all, my perceived mandate as a physician initially forbade any consideration of discontinuing the respirator. This was the same view that had governed my thinking twenty-five years ago in Steve's case. Much as my instincts as a human being had empathized with both of their respective requests, I simply could not venture on my own where David no longer feared to tread. Yet by now, the secular rules of the game in medical ethics were more clearly defined: based upon the hallowed principle of autonomy, it was ultimately his decision to make. In the end, David chose to take the road less traveled.

Far from surrendering to the "dark side of his heart" as Steve had done absent Christ in his life, David was answering his own call to God's eternal Kingdom. Few travelers who have crossed this divide, I suspect, have been more at peace with that than this trusting servant. The celebration of his eternal life among those family members left behind, who gathered around the bedside at David's passing, stood in embarrassing contrast to those "healers" among us, who sensed only defeat. For we were the one's "left behind" in our own wilderness of intensive-care protocols and machines that had assumed a life (albeit all too often futile) of their own. As for David, he had entered the Kingdom escorted by a supporting cast of Believers, who marked his crossing in celebration of life everlasting.

Contrast that experience with what the secular world perceives today to be a far more "realistic" view of death, as graphically portrayed by one very able and well-credentialed spokesperson for the medical profession:

> Katie is not in her body anymore. She's behind me, up there above me, and floating. Her body is just a shell now. At that point, everything was different than it had been before I first went to her side—I had an awareness that my daughter had died. I felt she was no longer in her body, that she was somewhere else...."
>
> "The look on her face was a look of utter surprise—a combination of being helpless, confused, and surprised, but definitely not a look of horror, and I remember being relieved that it wasn't.... Do you know what it looked like? It looked like a *release*. After seeing him attack her that way, it gave me a sense of peace to see that look of release. She looked surprised but not terrified.... My friend Susan saw that too...and when I told her it was a look of release, she said, 'That's it, you're right!'

So did Sherwin B. Nuland recount a mother's description of her daughter's death at the hand of a knife-wielding madman in his best-seller *How We Die: Reflections of Life's Final Chapter*. Now,

I don't mind admitting that my immediate response as a Christian to the subtitle was "Final? Sez who?" That was the first of a whole host of questions left unasked—much less answered—reflecting the author's secular perspective, which I too had once embraced while writing a similar book. My effort proved to be a monumental failure, not so much because I failed to ask the right questions, but because I was unable to reconcile these insoluble dilemmas for those left behind. Now, six years after becoming a born-again Christian, I think I know why: the same humanist mind-set that Nuland and I once shared is simply inadequate for the task.

True, what he portrays as a "classic description of death" as seen through the eyes of a grieving loved-one bears the authoritative stamp of empiric observation. That is as far as the author takes it, however; perhaps with good reason. For one thing, Nuland is of Jewish heritage. The perspective of an evangelical Christian is radically different. Some readers would view the last half of the mother's description as reflecting a "release" of the soul at the time of death. This adds a whole new dimension to Nuland's interpretation that a "physiological release of endorphins" had been responsible for the daughter's appearance—not to mention its ultimate implications that embracing a purely scientific view ignores. My point is this: a theistic perspective, which the mother's account also supports, is no less valid than a naturalist's explanation.

From the standpoint of sales, of course, Nuland didn't need to address the issue of souls. His book was assured of becoming a bestseller, in part, because it reflected the mind-set of the broad majority of readers who share his life's view. Yet the author's justification for ignoring the reality of life after death is arguably short-sighted, if not rather sad; for Nuland's intent was limited to providing "objective data" to prepare man for his own death as an *end point*— rather than accepting death as a *new beginning*, as Christians do.

His motive is no less suspect from the theist's perspective: "to soften one's final hours;" to see to it that we live our lives so as to "make sense of our deaths." What Nuland was encouraging his readers to do is build monuments to themselves while they still can, and to "take control" of their death once they begin the downhill slide. That preoccupation he identifies as man's "only realistic hope," found solely in the message of what our lives have been, as "something we can achieve." This is really to admit, however,that the only "permanent" attribute of being human, absent Christ, is our own mortality; that we will disappear and (horror of horrors!) soon be forgotten.

There is a touch of irony for myself in Nuland's self-perception as a "demythologizer." He warns us that the comfort and peace people experience at the time of death is "vastly overrated," and that we should not be "lulled" into unjustified expectations. That's ironic, because I too had cultivated a modest reputation in the academic world during my first life writing books for the purpose of debunking myths of a different sort: those related to the compromised health of past world leaders.[55] Yet to paraphrase the apostle Paul in gentler terms, I now consider those works insignificant and immaterial compared to having gained Christ in my life. In one sense, however, they did have some redeeming value; having later applied the same scientific and historical methodology (not "mythodology") to the Bible, I found nothing but affirmation of its timeless truths.[56]

That stands in equally ironic contrast to Nuland's assessment of any contribution the famed medical missionary Robert Livingston may have made to our understanding of death: "Long ago before science intervened, most would agree with Livingston's assessment concerning a 'merciful provision' by our benevolent Creator for lessening the pain of death.... [Yet] absent a supreme leap of psychic vision, he could not have foreseen the discovery of such [a biochemical phenomenon as endorphins] that now explains this." Invoking anything else but physiology, you see, is wishful thinking. To Nuland's way of thinking, "we must believe all things are possible, including God [!], because some of us *wish to be convinced*" (emphasis mine).

As "wishful thinkers," Christians would respectfully offer a whole host of rebuttals on Dr. Livingston's behalf to such condescending commentary:

1. Whether "leaps of psychic vision" or scientific hypotheses, neither are all-inclusive. Endorphins are real, but just a

small part of the picture. At best, medical science can only speculate as to what lies behind the veil of God's activity at the time of death;

2. The fact of the matter is, it's very dangerous *not* to "wish to be convinced," if we have been made in our Creator's image and offered reconciliation with Him for eternity;

3. I too have observed suffering and dying on the ward, and my own experience with respect to Believers who face either is diametrically opposed to Nuland's assertion that "most simply do not handle it well";

4. Which merely underscores the obvious: the truth lies in the *patient's* perspective and what faith he or she brings to the table—not Nuland's, nor even my own, for that matter. Granted, as physicians we may have been at the bedside; yet we've not been "there." Certainly that's what my Hispanic patient, David, and a whole host of God's saints who have crossed the Great Divide would tell us;

5. As for "falling prey to false hopes," the intent of this work is to affirm that just such expectations as Nuland decries are *entirely justified* within their proper context; and last;

6. To be "convinced" at the moment one faces death is hardly enough; confession and affirmation by way of commitment beforehand to all that Jesus promises is a necessary part of the Christian life (which happens to *include* physiologic death) from beginning to end.

Nuland's denigration of former giants of the profession extends to Sir William Osler, who also happened to have been a professed Christian and saint in his own right. Dr. Osler's painful death was alleged to have contradicted all of his own studies of patients that died gracefully and peacefully. To which the Christian again would gently reply: "But what, sir, do you know of Osler's soul?" Or, for that matter, of Jesus' suffering during His crucifixion? No doubt Christ Himself felt the same sense of contradiction and abandonment on the cross. Yet that, as history indisputably attests, was hardly the end of the story. Nor should it be for us— and, in fact, never is for the Believer.

Perhaps subconsciously, Nuland's professional life's view betrays a far too prevalent motive among physicians today: that the most rewarding aspect of healing is derived "not from the works of our heart but from those of our intellects"; that our self-worth as physicians revolves around solving what he terms "The Riddle." To his way of thinking, that entails wrestling with a diagnosis and instituting an appropriate treatment. This remains the "foremost challenge" in medicine today.

Having catered to that belief at one point in my own career, the fact of the matter is that, now, I could not disagree more. Nurturing one's professional "self-image" is one thing; acknowledging that we are created in the image of God, and adhering to that standard, is another—and a far more ennobling (and enabling) charge. The first is self-absorption; the second, self-actualization. That's what distinguishes the Curer from the Carer: the short-term gain (and game[57]) from the eternal goal. Christ Himself implied as much by healing the paralytic, not so much for the Cure as for the Care, when He affirmed: "So that you may know the Son of Man has authority to forgive sins, take your mat and go home" (Matthew 9:6).

On one matter, at first glance, we both seem to agree. In Nuland's own words: "the greater humility that should have come with increased knowledge [for the physician] is replaced instead by medical hubris." This he terms our "loadstone" as applied scientists. As one among many in the body of Christ who also happen to be care-givers, the proverbial Biblical "millstone" would seem more appropriate, threatening to drag us down to the depths. Rather than the hubris that prompts us to take credit for our few victories and to walk away from our failures, the Christian physician would emphasize the humility that keeps his ego in balance and his work in perspective: to God goes the glory for our healings, and to our patients His comfort when we fail.

Perhaps the Christian philosopher Ravi Zacharias most succinctly addressed the crux of the issue for physicians: to first understand one's *identity* before God. We have been chosen by the Lord, first and foremost, as followers of Him. Our profession just happens to be the *context* in which we have been placed. If we gain our identity from our relationship with God (and only secondarily from the work to which He has called us), we will always have a higher call to sustain us, rather than risk being swallowed up by the ebb and flow of success or failure. Otherwise we find ourselves manipulating the options to suit our own predispositions (which are equally subject to flux), and suffering accordingly—as do our patients, who depend on us.

In much the same way, death does not necessarily "belong to the dying and to those who love them," as Nuland would have us believe. Ultimately, death belongs to God for His divine purpose of reconciling ourselves to Him in eternity—not to mention that He loves us far more than any human being possibly could. That applies to the prayers we offer, which Nuland asserts "may not be possible to answer." For the humanist who asks them from the vantage point of himself as the center of the universe, no doubt that is true—because those prayers will be self-centered, not God-centered. Accordingly, the limited answers one receives simply reflect the motivation he or she brings to such an exercise as "making a wishlist." Yet God answers all prayers of the Believer. Perhaps not always when we would like (or even to our liking), though that misses the point of prayer to begin with: aligning our mind-set with God's will, so as to nurture a relationship that will be eternal. That is why Christians are fond of saying, "life is fragile; handle with prayer."

This matter of wishlists brings to mind Nuland's perspective of the deathbed scene: "for most, an image of wishfulness, an ideal...but [one] usually not obtained." Not so for Christians, as my own experience attests! Their faith in a God-centered life puts to rest any wish-list of a self-centered existence. Rather, they believe in what they hope for, and are certain of what they cannot see. After all, God has already given them eternal life through Christ's finished work on the cross. That's His promise—and all the proof they require.

Not that Nuland doesn't acknowledge some "form" of God in positing his own wishlist when he quotes the prayer of poet Rainer Maria Rilke: "Oh Lord, give each of us his own death." In large measure, that's the last we hear of the only perspective that really matters. Whereas Nuland argues that to "give each his own death." depends solely on mankind's educated choices rather than God's sovereign grace, what both he and the poet are really appealing to is God's *mercy*, the true arbiter of the matter.

This brings us full circle to a reconsideration of the visage of "release" that characterized the young girl at the moment she died. I don't have any quarrel with the physiology of an "endorphin surge" in Nuland's explanation. Lest we forget: Jesus was also a human being while still on the cross, and subject to the same physiologic response. Perhaps a precipitate increase in these circulating hormones under the duress of scourging and crucifixion did play some role during those final hours when He bore the stress of dying so stoically. Yet endorphins most assuredly do *not* explain such phrases in the mother's description of her daughter (and seconded by an independent observer) as "not in her body anymore"; "behind me, up there above me, floating"; "no longer in her body…[but] somewhere else."

For those with eyes to see and ears to hear as their Creator intended, what is at issue here is whether the mother is simply describing the effects of an endorphin release within a dying body, or a peace that passes all understanding as the living soul is released for eternity. Do I accept the latter view simply because I now have "spirit-filled" vision? Or is this perspective of death more universal than most experts are willing to acknowledge? Compelling questions, to be sure—because none of us, as yet, has *been* there. As such, the gulf separating the naturalist's "death's view" from the theist's could not be more starkly drawn. For Nuland would have us believe that death is an end, experienced alone by man, through nature's laws, to be orchestrated for his benefit in the end. Yet for the Christian, death is a beginning, experienced with Christ, through His crucifixion, for our reconciliation with God in eternity.

The chasm separating the two perspectives can be summarized even more succinctly when it comes to proposing alternative explanations for the young girl's appearance at the time of her death. To quote Nuland: "I am convinced that nature stepped in and provided exactly the right spoonful of medication to give a measure of tranquility to a dying child." The Christian would respond differently: "I am convinced that God stepped in and provided the ultimate sacrifice of His Son to give total comfort and security to an eternal spirit."

Granted, this begs the question that cynics are bound to ask following such a sweeping propsition: am I espousing this merely to validate myself among my Christian peers? Though the secular mind never sees such evidence of God's providence, people of faith seem to stumble across His involvement everywhere. Perhaps more than is justified. Yet what makes my perspective somewhat unique is that I've lived (and suffered) on both sides of the issue. In the end, the evidence spoke for itself—loud and clear.

Though Nuland implies that many of his own speculations must be taken on "faith," and even concedes that "some of my proof-demanding colleagues will no doubt find fault with my assumptions," I, for one, do not—as far as they go. I too have witnessed the same type of endorphin-engendered phenomena in the emergency room and on the ward. What I *do* find fault with, however, is his myopic life's view that fails to take into account faith of a more literal sort. Whereas his perspective may find acceptance on the naturalist's terms, it is antithetical to theists who know the living God personally. And that, for the Christian, is a faith—a "release"—worth dying for with serenity.

Ironically, that begins with death of a different sort for the Christian—dying to self and depending on Jesus. For one cannot call on Him unless convicted. This then leads to our confession that Christ alone is the answer, made possible through His Father's grace. That message is the very heart of Romans, and one that Paul defends so eloquently with proofs taken from the Old Testament (the very Scripture of Nuland's own heritage).

What Paul was saying is that to confess we must first *believe*. This represents the heart of what I've labored to say in these pages: that God ultimately created everything for the good of man, the latter of whom (as a fallen creation in his own right) is as limited in his perceptions of suffering and dying as are unbelievers today—and I myself, before embracing the Living God. That belief in particular, like faith in general, centers on two words: Jesus Christ.

Christians know that, because the Jesus of history can be reconciled with the Christ of our faith. We have His assurance that He is as much the answer at the *end* as during the time we are each allotted during His Seventh Day of Creation. Because death is only the beginning. Just ask my Dad....

Verdict

Post-Mortem

Sharing a personal relationship with the living God is, at once, His unmerited gift to us and our intended choice for Him. Perhaps there is no better place to plumb the depths of what that relationship can be than when and where it all started: on the Sixth Day of Creation in Genesis, when God first "divined" us. By His own declaration, everything was good. The Potter and His clay were as one. We were family.

Then we sinned on the Seventh Day, breaking faith with God—and His heart in the process. That's when He began to intervene in our lives as a concerned Father. Despite that, the remainder of Genesis is a sordid tale of one failed relationship after another— failures that have been repeated through all generations to the present day.

A great beginning; intimations of a terrible end! Now if *you* were God, what would you have done with these sinners originally created in the very likeness of yourself? Expunge them and wipe the slate clean? Probably. Yet God's ways are not man's ways. Instead of destroying mankind, He chose to give us all a new beginning by calling a man named Abram[58] to leave his home for the Promised Land.

Consider the profound implications of this singular response of but one man to God's Word. From the seed of Abraham's obedience emerged the Jewish remnant, then the timeless truth of the Bible, and ultimately our Savior. Where would we be today without that single unselfish act? More to the point, what road map did God provide for him to follow? In a word, *none*. He had to walk in faith alone.

Things are different today. Unlike Abraham, we have been given so many signposts to guide our way, yet we still manage to miss the turnoff God intended us to take. "No matter," we rationalize. In the early going, the detours we follow seem harmless enough, what with all those mesmerizing billboards littering the secular landscape that tell us what to value, how to behave, or which Siren beckons. Eventually, however, harsh reality sinks in: we're lost! We simply can't get to where God intends us to be by continuing down the wrong road. This means retracing our steps and returning to the crossroads where we left the Lord (or never acknowledged Him to begin with) and went our own way. In that sense, the Christian walk is a series of new beginnings, what Jesus termed "repentance": turning from self and toward God.

For most of us, just as it was for Abraham, that can be an intensely painful experience. It's like returning down a dark tunnel—a tunnel of "brokenness"—without knowing what we will find (no, what we will *be*) at the other end. All too often God has to break us up into pieces and shove us through the filter of this narrow aperture in order for His likeness to emerge. The detritus of our past—a career set-back, an unintended divorce—litters the tunnel behind us like so many roadblocks, as reminders that we cannot pass that way again. What we discover instead is that there is more to repentance than "turning" from self and towards God. True repentance means *dying to self* within the tunnel and embracing Jesus at the other end. That's what the journey is for.

Because we left; that's why He came. Taking us by the hand, Jesus ushers us into the same sacred relationship that Abraham once acknowledged as a covenant between mentor and friend, master and servant, father and son: specifically, the Lord promises to reveal the Father's intent for our lives and to share His love with us from beginning to end.

That comes with an obligation on our part to nurture the relationship. Whereas the living God reveals Himself today through nature, the Word, and His Son, our intended response *to* Him entails awe and wonder of the first, obedience to the second, and imitation of the third at the behest of the Holy Spirit. From Abraham's day until the time of Moses, the security of God's people was to be found in His presence: billowing smoke by day, and a pillar of fire by night. Yet today, day or night, His invisible Holy Spirit is present in each of us. This is God's way of telling us that we have even less excuse now to ignore the tunnel and continue down the wrong road.

The problem from the beginning, you see, is that we have been given special gifts of free will and choice as His children—made as we are in His image. For God knew that without choice there can be no such thing as love. To be sure, not everyone in the Father's Kingdom thought this gift was a good idea at the time. Consider those skeptical angels standing aghast on the Sixth Day of Creation while God played in the dirt, molding His special piece of clay. One holy wag probably had the audacity to whisper in the Creator's ear, "Free will? Surely you jest! What if your special creation chooses not to enter into a relationship with you?" To which God prophetically, if wistfully, replied: "Some will; most won't."[59]

Therein lies modern man's proverbial "thorn [of] the flesh"— what philosophers term "humanism"—born of the eighteenth century Enlightenment with the best of mortal intentions, yet bludgeoned to death by the "Be All You Can Be" generation of today. For most of our choices continue to be poor ones. That's the nature of the beast. From the lineage of Adam and Eve down through the centuries, sin has passed from one generation to the next. It's part of our genetic makeup, shot through with self-destructive "mutations" far removed from God's holy genotype.

Now, insofar as we have been given minds to exercise free will and make choices, what we do with such gifts cannot help but follow a logical progression:

> Sow a thought, reap an action.
> Sow an action, reap a habit.
> Sow a habit, reap a character.
> Sow a character, reap a destiny.

Yet when we look into the mirror, what do we see? Probably an image that we vaingloriously seek to preserve by building our own Towers of Babel. We want to play God without paying Him the compliment of following the only blueprint He gave us in the flesh. For history (with a small "h") is replete with people like you and me who have labored in vain to build monuments to ourselves apart from God. If that's *sad* history to read, it's also *bad* history to study—examining man's Towers of Babel as if they were worthy of scrutiny, if not imitation.

The truth of the matter is, *His* Story is all that matters. That's what God was proclaiming when He gave us an exemplary set of rules for righteous living—not only to protect us, but to prove His omniscience and dispel any illusions we may have concerning our own. Having failed God's original commandments time and again, we remain recalcitrant pupils despite the reality of absolute truth staring us in the face. If you doubt that, then consider what our secular conventions have done to His Holy Commandments:

The Ten Commandments of God's Eternal Kingdom	vs.	The Ten Conventions of Post-Modern Society
-what to believe in and trust for all time		-what to conform with and get by for now
-an *absolute* code of conduct for righteous living		-a *relative* codicil of behavior for self-preservation
-timeless: applies to any age		-ephemeral: defined by the age
-a commitment by one's own choice as intended by God		-an anachronism by its very nature as rationalized by man.

By virtue of being honored as His Commandments, the first four of the Ten center on God. By virtue of being accepted as conventions, our respective contrapositions focus upon self. That's why the first three Commandments begin with "shall," as in "must"; the conventions with "should," as in "may."

I. "You shall have no other Gods before me"

vs.

"You should not impose God on others"

"I am Who I am"

-"I'm OK; you're OK."

-God created man *by* Himself, as a father begats a son in His own image

-man created God *for* Himself, as a sinecure to fulfill a psychological need

-God is the Creator of His universe

-man is the center of our universe

-God in Three Persons is the ultimate reality

-nature and its laws are the only reality

II. "You shall not make for yourself idols...nor worship them...for I am a jealous God"

vs.

"You should trumpet your own achievements...as a celebration of what mankind can do"

-all we have is God's to begin with; He has dominion over everything, including man

-modern technology puts out sacred fires; it shrinks the dominion of God and extends the domain of man

-we are all one body in Christ, who justified us as God's chosen

-we are as one with the interest group or subset that defines us

-only God is inerrantly good

-all men are inherently "good"

III. "You shall not misuse the name of the Lord your God"

vs.

"You should not misconstrue the person of Jesus for God"

-not what we do for God, but what He does through us

-not ascribing to God what he can do, but what nature does around us

-not what we say, but how we live, that "speaks" for God

-not preempting the right, as fundamentalists do, to "speak" for God

-Jesus is the answer

-so what's the question?

IV. "Remember the Sabbath and keep it Holy"	vs.	"Science is king; acknowledge its preeminence"
-take God at His Word; only He is omniscient		-take the experts' word for it; their insight is sufficient
-build altars to God that glorify His presence		-build monuments to yourself that justify your existence
-enter His "rest" to honor God		-indulge repose to "honor" yourself
-worship offers sacred community, bringing people to God, together		- "worship" belies secular convention, bringing people together, not to God

Which brings us back to those signposts God intends us to follow today, including an explanation of where they came from and how we can be assured they are a part of His divine plan. Look at it this way. With all due respect to God's Ten Commandments, before Abraham, man's old nature *knew* no law; after Christ, man's new nature *needed* no law, because it was written on our hearts by the Holy Spirit. The latter is synonymous with what C. S. Lewis terms the "Law of Human Nature," an inherent (and inerrant) sense of right and wrong. Here is a law that man certainly didn't make, but one he knows he ought to obey, because it was created and bequeathed by a mind infinitely greater than his own....

Look at it another way. As children we tried to please our parents—an absolute (if not infallible) standard of sorts—by floating our boats in their stream. As adults, we tack back and forth in uncharted oceans of uncertainty, driven by the whimsical winds of society. So what happens when those standards change, as they always do, and we're left as ships without compasses? When do we allow the Lord to seize the keel as we find ourselves tossed about amid swales of competing value systems? Only when we accept that a higher moral law exists, acknowledge Who created it, admit we have broken that law and are at odds with Him—then, and *only* then, will Christ calm the storm and Christianity finally speak to wayward man cast adrift in seas of relativism.

I learned that from firsthand experience. You may recall that my response to Steve's predicament was colored with post-modern buzzwords like "existential trials," "self-determination," and "guilt transfer." Yet I emerged from the second crisis of belief (mine, certainly not David's) with sacred perspectives that have withstood the test of time—truths like redemptive suffering, dying to self, and justification by grace through faith.

Given such unmerited grace, do you ever wonder why so many men in the Bible including kings such as Saul, David, and Solomon failed God in mid-life? I suspect it has something to do with our make-up before we allow ourselves to be made-over in His image. True, our Creator is always looking for clay to mold. Yet clay has no mind of its own—much less, a divine plan. That's a lesson I had to relearn in Brazil when I found myself "at sea" in the clinic as a member of the crew, instead of captain of the ship doing brain operations: something about God's plan, and not my own agenda....

Or yet another lesson, when I met the Lord face to face in El Salvador, and finally tumbled to the realization of what Jesus meant by the term "Son of Man." Wading one morning through a crush of grateful humanity as we arrived at the clinic, I was literally accosted by a wizened, toothless bag lady, who grabbed my hand and stuck it into the side pocket of her tattered jacket. Extracting what looked like a wrapped piece of candy, she guided my hands as I fumbled to remove the wrapper. Deeply moved by her gift, I interpreted this as an undeserved act of kindness shown to me in gratitude for what we were doing for her people. I nodded in appreciation and prepared to consume the tiny morsel—at which point she took my unwrapped treasure, belched loudly, and popped it into her mouth.

As it turned out, this was not my candy—but her medicine. Upon reflection, I realized that this humble soul was none other than Christ in disguise, bringing me down from my missionary pedestal. This had been Jesus' way of reminding me that I was there to serve Him through them. If that meant simply assisting an elderly woman whose hands were so gnarled by crippling arthritis that she could no longer unwrap her own medicine, then so be it—and the Lord be praised!

What made this encounter such a revelation was learning afterwards that the Hebrew word for "son" equates with "servant."[60] Now, a servant's function is to follow instructions; the master's role is to give directions—regardless of whether the latter appears as God's begotten Son or mankind's forgotten bag lady. Understood. Yet as Son of Man, Jesus also came to earth as Servant of Man. That service was paid in full on the cross. With complete justification, Jesus could proclaim, "It is finished." He had fulfilled His Father's command to the letter—and with His life.

Now is the time for each of us to do the same. As His disciples, the only justifiable standard of conduct worthy of Jesus is our best imitation of Him, Who made us. Once we have done all those things that He commanded, then we can proclaim (solely through His justification) that "we are but unprofitable servants. We have simply done what was our duty to do" (Luke 17:10). That is why He sent me to the missions field. Yet my story is not important; His is. May you discover this through yours. That's what the Seventh Day of Creation is all about.

Endnotes

1. Luke 14:25-35.
2. Matthew 19:16-21.
3. Matthew 12:34.
4. Ephesians 6:14-16.
5. Genesis 50:19-21. What was "it" specifically that God meant for good? "To accomplish what is now being done, the saving of many lives" (50:20). As applied to Eric's family and close friends, the salvations that have resulted are for eternity. See pp. 37-38 below.
6. This is a prevailing theme in chapter 9 of Romans, and a specific mandate in 1 Peter 2:9.
7. Philip Yancey refers to this as "the Great Reversal of God's Kingdom" in his critically acclaimed work *The Jesus I Never Knew*, Grand Rapids, Michigan: Zondervan Publishing House, p. 143.
8. Monica Hellwig, "Good News to the Poor: Do They Understand It Better?" Cited in *Tracing the Spirit*, Mahwah, New Jersey: Paulist Press, 1983, p. 145.
9. Matthew 7:14.
10. Judges 17:6.
11. C.S. Lewis, *Mere Christianity*, New York: Simon and Schuster, 1952, p. 155. It is fitting that Lewis titles the chapter from which this quote is taken as "The Obstinate Toy Soldiers."
12. Jeremiah 18:6.
13. Jeremiah 2:13.
14. Ezekiel 37:1.
15. Acts 17:22,24.
16. See below, pp. 95-98.
17. Matthew 4:23-25.
18. The parallel drawn is from Genesis 19, in which Lot had faced down a surly crowd of men demanding that he surrender two angels staying at his house for their own nefarious pleasures.
19. Mark 13:11.
20. See pp. 14-15 above.
21. Psalms 16:8,10.
22. Such failings are hardly confined to unseasoned missions teams and cynical government officials. Witness the experience of an unwed mother I subsequently ministered to in Guatemala, who was informed by her own pastor that she could not be baptized until her absentee mate agreed to marry her!

23. Sadly enough, he was instrumental in the split. Someone very close to me had initially misinterpreted my life's change, and conveyed her concerns to my "brother" in Christ while I was away. This information he thought my partners might like to know, despite having been given it in strict confidence. Their decision to terminate me was made within the very week of that disclosure. Once I was out of the picture, that allowed them to form their own partnership.

24. Matthew 11:28-30.

25. Matthew 5:11-12.

26. There have been twenty-five trips to date over a six-year period, during which I have *never* had one of my patients at home develop postoperative complications or problems that required my presence there. The Great Physician has met their every need in my absence. There is, quite simply, no other way to explain it. Contrast that with the only two times Vicki and I have tried to take a vacation, both of which required terminating the trip and returning home. Painful affirmation of a sort? Of course. Yet my wife's heart is so in tune with God's plan for our lives together that we accept this as a small price to pay for the privilege of sharing space and patients where He is working.

27. For a concise assessment of Cole's impact on other Christians, see Philip Yancey, *Soul Survivor*, New York, Doubleday, 2001, p. 110.

28. Ibid. p. 111.

29. Ibid. p. 116.

30. Luke 4:24.

31. Luke 6:20-23.

32. Luke 6:24-26.

33. Colossians 1:28.

34. Matthew 5:13.

35. Matthew 5:14-15.

36. Matthew 5:16.

37. That subsequently proved not to be as overly dramatized as one might imagine. A year after returning from Siberia I was sent a newspaper clipping detailing the deterioration of Russian infrastructure in general, and its transport vehicles in particular. The centerfold of the piece was a picture of a cargo plane that had crashed into a village, its tail jutting up amid the rubble. That was a protype of the very plane we had taken the year before! "Blessed are the merciful, for they shall be shown mercy." Thankfully, that had been manifested to us on this side of the Great Divide....

38. Luke 5:17-26.

39. John 14:27.

40. The term derives from the earliest missions experiences in China, where the people came to hear the message for the more palatable reward of receiving a free meal.

41. But not forever. God will not be mocked. A mere two years later, Jesus would reveal what the Father has in mind for Vietnam, one of the last remaining strongholds of Satan. That's when I returned to Danang. As events over our two-week mission there affirmed beyond doubt, the Lord intends to establish His beachhead in the heart of Vietnam, not in Hanoi as we mere mortals had once envisioned. The seeds planted in such a short period of time on behalf of His Kingdom were so prolific as to preclude their complete recounting here. For now, a paraphrase of John 21:25 must suffice: "Jesus did so many things while we were there that, if every one of them were written down, the whole world would not have room for the books that would be written." What's more, a month before submitting this manuscript for

publication, I received an e-mail from Hanoi, finally inviting me to return. "Wait on the Lord!" Everything in His own time....

42. This is a prevailing theme of the Pentateuch, and one that has been validated throughout the history of both Judaism and Christianity. Not only has Judaism survived on God alone; Christians have stood on Jesus' promise for two thousand years that He indeed is the "Bread of Life."

43. Or so it seems to those of us in short-term missions, who are just "passing through." Randomly casting our nets in this huge ocean of humanity is no substitute for those patient missionaries who wait in one spot and let the schools of fish seeking living waters come to them. The experience of Sebastian's family in Byelorus is a case in point. Before they were expelled from the country during the anti-Christian pogrom of the mid-1990s, they had spent four years developing a Bible school. Today, despite their absence, that school is now *700* strong and its numbers growing daily!

44. John 1:1.

45. Philippians 2:6-7.

46. See below, p. 130.

47. For further reflections on suffering and death from the Christian perspective, see "Death: An End or a New Beginning?" below, p. 127.

48. Harold Kushner, *When Bad Things Happen to Good People*. New York: Avon Books, 1983.

49. Luke 4:18-21.

50. Bert E. Park. *Catastrophic Illness and the Family*. Boston: Christopher Publishing House, 1992

51. Joseph Conrad, *Heart of Darkness*. New York: New American Library, 1983, p. 147.

52. A special hospital bed formerly used for patients with spinal cord injuries.

53. Conrad, *Heart of Darkness*, p. 144

54. Ibid

55. Bert E. Park, *The Impact of Illness on World Leaders*. Philadelphia: University of Pennsylvania Press, 1986; and *Ailing, Aging, Addicted: Studies of Compromised Leadership*. Lexington: University Press of Kentucky, 1993.

56. Bert E. Park, *Meeting Jesus on the Road: His Story, From Creation to Apocalypse*, Enumclaw: WinePress Publishers, 2003.

57. Insofar as today's physician is said to be "caught up in the wonders of modern science," he walks away when his power over the disease process no longer exists. Nuland correctly perceives this as a vainglorious "fantasy of controlling nature" that lies at the heart of modern medicine; vainglorious, because "nature always wins." And so it does; yet only to fulfill God's eternal purpose for each Believer's life. For the physician who inevitably loses in this struggle of postponing death, the dying then becomes the important thing from Nuland's perspective. To which the Christian physician would respond: It's eternal life through Christ that supersedes all.

58. Soon to be renamed "Abraham," once God established His covenant with him.

59. Max Lucado. "When You Can't Hide Your Mistakes."

60. Psalm 2:7 (see end note in NIV text).

Trial by Fire
Order Form

Postal orders: Christian Surgical Foundation
6319 S. Creeks Edge Court
Springfield, MO 65721

Telephone orders: 417-882-3569

E-mail orders: BEParkneuro@cs.com

Please send *Trial by Fire* to:

Name: _____

Address: _____

City: _____ State: _____

Zip: _____

Telephone: (_____) _____

Book Price: $10.95

Shipping: $3.00 for the first book and $1.00 for each additional book to cover shipping and handling within US, Canada, and Mexico. International orders add $6.00 for the first book and $2.00 for each additional book.

Or order from:
ACW Press
85334 Lorane Hwy
Eugene, OR 97405

(800) 931-BOOK

or contact your local bookstore